Held

A Story of Survival, Faith, and Redemption

ALORA STONE

Small Mountain Writing

Held
by Alora Stone
Copyright ©2026 Alora Stone

ISBN 978-1-63360-354-7

All rights reserved. This book is protected under the copyright laws of the United States of America. This book may not be copied or reprinted for commercial gain or profit.

For Worldwide Distribution   Printed in the USA

Urban Press
PO Box 5044
Williamsburg, VA 23188
757.808.5776
www.urbanpress.us

He said: "Listen, King Jehoshaphat and all who live in Judah and Jerusalem! This is what the Lord says to you: 'Do not be afraid or discouraged because of this vast army. For the battle is not yours, but God's.'"
– 2 Chronicles 20:15

The names and identifying details of some individuals have been changed to protect their privacy.

DEDICATION

To my husband, my greatest supporter and constant encourager, who gave me the courage to be vulnerable and to share our story.

To my brave and beautiful daughters, who championed me every step of the way—encouraging me to keep writing, to keep growing, and to always stand up for myself.

To my best friend who walked this journey with me for the last 30 years; you are truly a gift to me.

And to all who are currently on a journey in pursuit of redemption—may you know that you are not alone, and that hope is closer than you think.

Above all, I dedicate this book to Jesus—who has rescued me more times than I can count, who has shown me what true love is, and who has held me my entire life, promising never to let me go.

ACKNOWLEDGEMENTS

Throughout this journey, there have been many special people who encouraged and supported me, and I would like to acknowledge them here.

To my prayer warriors who engaged in the battle with me—without the prayers of the saints rising up, I know this project would not have been accomplished. To the mental health professionals who played a role in my healing, both physical and emotional, thank you for providing a safe place to process, heal, and continue forward.

To my children, who read this book and gave me their blessing to share our story—without your approval, this book would not exist. To the love of my life, my husband of nearly 27 years, who has stood by my side every step of the way—your love, acceptance, and grace have shaped the person I have become. Without your encouragement, my voice may have remained silenced.

And above all, to my loving Savior and Friend—there are no words to fully express my gratitude. You continually lift me up, redeeming the parts of me I once believed were useless. Without Your forgiveness and unconditional love, I would still be at the bottom of a river.

Introduction

*"I can't die, I'm only 18 years old...
please save me God!"*

These were the words I screamed in my mind as I sat trapped underwater in my car unable to break free from my seatbelt. I frantically grabbed for anything to release me but was unsuccessful. Doing its job to the bitter end, the seatbelt secured me in place, dangling me upside down as if to defy gravity. Discombobulated and lacking air, I closed my eyes. The last chapter of my life had suddenly appeared out of nowhere. Without any warning, the last sentence was spoken. The last cry for help was muffled under the water. The last breath of life was exhaled. Or at least that's what I thought.

They say when you have a near-death experience, your life passes before your eyes. And one would categorize this as a near-death experience. However, my story took an unexpected turn. Instead of succumbing to death, I found new life as I was lifted out of the waters. The fall, the crash, the shattered glass, the water, the sinking were all real but none of it secured a place in my memory. The evidence pointed to the reality of the car accident but the only thing I remembered was the indescribable, supernatural grip of my heavenly Father as I fell, crashed, and sank. This was a Father I had abandoned.

I don't know how long I was underwater, and my memory is void of the actual crash but the moments that followed will forever be etched into my mind.

Coming out of the water was no different than jumping off the diving board and returning to the surface—no gasping for air, no frantic flailing of limbs as if running from attackers. There was nothing but a calm pull from the river's current onto an island in the middle of the river. Gingerly pulling myself up to my feet, I looked out and saw the rear left tire sticking out as if to usher reality into view. Through the grid of shock and adrenaline, I instinctively knew I needed to get help. And as if my year of rebellion and abandonment never happened, I called on Jesus to help me. Knowing full well he saved me from the water, I had courage to get back in and make my way to the cliff's edge. I knew I needed to get back to the road and flag someone down. So, I made my way through the water and up the cliff.

To understand my rebellion and ultimately my fall, both figuratively and literally, you must know my story before that dreadful beautiful day—a story I ironically was trying to end at every twist and turn. The parallels of drowning in my car and drowning in life were remarkable. My story is still being written almost 30 years later. And though I would love to say that being rescued by God ended my rebellion forever, it didn't. It did, however, set the direction of my life on a different path.

On this new path, I began to live for other reasons. In this new direction, I began to discover who God truly made me to be. And along the journey, I realized that God was just getting started with revealing who He is. This roller coaster called life has been amazing—the hills, the valleys, and everything in between.

I hope my story will encourage you to always remember that whenever you feel like you are in the battle alone, God is nearby. It may seem like he is hiding, distant, or just gone but the truth is you are held—He's right there beside you. And it's in these moments where you need to trust His words over your feelings. And His words are this: "The Lord himself goes before you and will be with you; He will never leave you nor forsake you. Do not be afraid; do not be discouraged" (Deuteronomy 31:8).

Alora Stone
February 2026

chapter 1

My Secret Life

A year before my accident, I had been secretively living with bulimia for two-and-a-half years. At first, I loved this covert existence, something that was just mine. It was a fantasy life that gave me hope and an identity. It offered me something I craved but never knew I needed—an exit, a way out. But after time, the sneaking around and lying started to give way and interfere with my ability to function. I had constant anxiety about being found out for fear of ridicule or worse yet, to have it be taken away from me. But the effects of its grip were becoming too much to bear.

I decided I would release some of the pressure and tell my sister, Lauren. I felt I could trust her, but I was wrong. She demanded I tell my parents, or she would. I still remember the day I told my mother.

"Mom, I've been struggling with bulimia for over two years. I'm sorry." I said, uncertain of how she would respond.

"Ok, well, just don't do it again."

And that was that. In that instant, the

responsibility of my life and my choices shifted onto her because she now knew. If I died from this disease, she was at fault because she had knowledge of what her child was doing. She was just as culpable for my consequences as she would be if she allowed her toddler to run around the house with scissors. I truly believed this and because of that, I made myself believe I was invincible–and my reckless decisions would back up my belief.

Eating disorders were not a thing back in the early '90s. Sure movie stars and singers would succumb to such a selfish demise, but common folk? We didn't know anyone who had this kind of plague. So, the only thing my parents could think to do was outsource my problem to a hospital. What my parents hoped would help me became the impetus for further self-destruction. As if being the new girl in a small town of 300 and a pastor's kid wasn't enough, my secret life was broadcast to the world, leaving me exposed and threatened.

Lost Girl

I longed for acceptance and approval, and I wanted to matter. I'm not sure I would've recognized what that looked like, but I knew life would be better if I had it. One day while in the hospital I received a big envelope from my English teacher. Inside contained over a dozen hand-written get-well cards from my classmates. As I read over each one, I cherished every word beautifully written. For the first time, I was seen. The well wishes and prayers committed over me that day filled my heart. But I would soon learn after being released that the cards were a mandatory homework assignment from the teacher which was met with grunts and half-hearted cooperation. I was devastated. If it was possible to think any lower of myself, I did. But buried beneath my fleshly ambition was actually God's love, acceptance, and approval of me.

My eating disorder, which I would later refer to as ED, was the only real friend I had. No one knew me like ED. And no one had my back like ED. Sure he tempted me to eat, justifying it was okay since I had successfully starved myself that day, only to shame me for it the moment I finished my last bite.

And though he was my abuser, he always provided a way out. After shaming me for having no willpower, he would remind me of the cure. I could purge it all and instantly erase my failures. My relationship with my disorder mirrored Stockholm Syndrome. Even after I was admitted into the hospital, ED played a big role in my destruction. And the sneaking around game we bonded over continued well into the weeks I found myself locked up.

I had to participate in individual, group, and family counseling almost daily. The counselors would constantly try to provoke and incite a reaction from me. But I was dead inside, and there wasn't going to be a resurrection anytime soon. They tried their best to get me angry by saying I had pent up anger towards my parents and to just let it out. I guess they thought if I could release all my emotions, then we could start to put the pieces together. But I was empty.

"I'm not angry," I would respond.

"Of course, you are. That's why you have an eating disorder," they would counter.

I felt nothing. No pain, no desire to blame anyone, no explanation for the life I found myself in. Conversely, I didn't feel joy, peace, or happiness either (the emotions I would've spent a million dollars to have).

The program set us up to fail. Every day they provided therapy, enforced rules, and created an unrealistic environment in which we would never find outside those four walls. They told us when, where, and what to eat. I couldn't go to the bathroom for at least an hour after eating. And when I would escape to my quarters, I was met with a big empty room that smelled as sterile as it looked.

In their attempt to help me, they stole my freedom. The only thing I had been living for had been exposed and taken from me. The irony was in the fact that one who feels they have no control will begin to control their food and diet. I was an untamed wild animal who had been captured and chained up. And so, when I met some other inmates who shared some of their tricks with me of how to drop weight fast, I counted the days until I would be released and able to implement these new ideas. What I didn't know at the time was these new tricks would become like grenades threatening to destroy my life.

Chapter 2

The Love Of A Grandmother

Graduation came a month later. I made plans to move in with my grandparents in California. I had spent the previous 17 years following other people's demands, expectations, and suggestions without giving much thought to what I wanted. The lack of involvement in my own life left me asking myself, "Now what?" I didn't know which direction to go but I knew moving in any direction was better than not moving at all. I anticipated a new place would lead to a path of happiness and completeness. So, I headed out, with my new tricks in one hand and grenades in the other.

My grandparents were the best. I always knew I was welcome at their house. My grandfather was not as emotionally involved as my grandma, but he was a man from a different generation. Thankfully what my grandfather lacked, my grandmother made up for in spades. She was my rock. I knew anytime I would visit her, I would receive endless hugs, kisses, and love.

Ingrid was her name. She was born and raised in Norway until she came to Ellis Island with her family when she was just 11 years old. Her family settled in Santa Elia, CA, 55 miles north of San Francisco, the home to wine country. For miles and miles, you could see beautiful vineyards and historic chateaus as you drove through Napa Valley to get to Grandma's house.

However, Ingrid had been in a prison of her own in the early days. Married to an abusive alcoholic, she practically raised my father by herself. One day she got the courage to leave her husband. Wanting my father to still have contact with his dad, she would line up visits for him to pick up my dad for the day. But many times, he wouldn't show up and she would end up wiping away tears from my father's cheeks as they sat on the front porch. "I'm sorry, sweetheart. Maybe he lost track of time at work. Maybe next week he can come and pick you up." After a while Grandma stopped making excuses and stopped making plans. She wondered if God would wipe away her tears.

When my father was 10, Grandma met Henry. He was so good to her. He called her Dolly and treated her like a princess. They married and raised my dad together. Henry became the vice president of a title company which provided a good living for them. They enjoyed yearly vacations but always made family a priority. Every summer my parents would drive six hours from a small fishing town on the California/Oregon border to Santa Elia and drop us kids off for a month to stay with them. And now as I made the move back to Grandma's, I anticipated receiving her love.

I arrived at my grandparents' house weighing 110 pounds on a 5'6" frame. I was very sick but didn't realize it at the time. All I knew, or better yet all I wanted to know, was to be in a place where no one knew me. I was so exhausted from being the news of the day. Here, I could just be a girl looking to start my life.

I was given my own bedroom and was told I could stay as long as I wanted. As I walked into the bedroom I had spent countless days running around in years earlier, I recalled the days my sisters and I jumped on the beds laughing so hard we almost peed our pants. Emptying my suitcases and filling the armoire drawers, I remembered the letters I once found in those same dresser drawers from my father to my grandma when he was in Vietnam fighting for the freedoms I had been given.

Anytime we stayed at Grandma's house, I had to sleep on the couch. This bedroom only had two beds and I was the youngest of three daughters. So naturally, I would be forced to sleep on the couch. But now this bedroom, this bed, was all mine. I felt like a princess. And for the first time in a long time, I felt something. I felt love.

Back To Work

Then out of the blue, the feelings of love were interrupted by the mirror. "You have work to do! You are still so fat. It's time to try out the new tricks you learned in the hospital." Searching frantically for a scale, I uncovered Grandma's in her bedroom and stepped on it. Believing the weight of my oxygen would add another pound, I held my breath and looked down. The scale always had fighting words and today was no different. The scale and the mirror were the ones really in charge, and they were never satisfied, never impressed. They spoke all right, but it was always words of hate. They were there to motivate me, to beat me into submission.

The next day I implemented my newfound ideas not realizing that I just removed the pin in the grenade. My mind was hijacked with the idea to restrict food so I wouldn't have to throw up anymore. I had grown weary of the bulimic cycle and just wanted to eat enough food to survive. After doing this for a few weeks, a night I will never forget came and changed the course of my life forever, a night when God called on my assigned heavenly angel to stand guard.

Though I knew some of the choices I was making surrounding my health weren't good, like going two days without eating, I continued. I loved the payoff. I was indeed dropping weight with my new tricks. I knew I just needed to get my body to a place of not craving food any longer and I could just maintain with minimal intake. So one night, after my grandparents had gone to bed, I started to read a book I had checked out at the library about eating disorders.

Scanning over the table of contents, I found the chapter on anorexia. This was the newest form of ED I had been playing around with. It was a lot less messy, and the results were what I was looking for. But I noticed I was more fearful when I played with anorexia fire. As I found the chapter I was looking for, I began to read about the deadly consequences of anorexia. I knew about the erosion of the esophagus and losing teeth due to acidic corrosion from throwing up. But the effects from anorexia seemed to be more final, more lethal. I read about heart failure and organs being starved of nutrition and shutting down. My heart started to race, and my breathing became labored. I began to hyperventilate and couldn't catch my breath. I was lightheaded and dizzy. I literally thought I was going to die.

Rushing into Grandmother's room, hands clinching my chest, I shrieked, "Grandma, I can't breathe!"

"Oh my gosh, Alora, sit down. Henry, Henry, wake up," Grandma screamed racing for the phone to dial 9-1-1.

"Yes, this is Ingrid. My granddaughter can't breathe. Please come quickly!" is all my grandmother could get out.

Already mentally and emotionally dead, all I could think about was the two-liter diet soda I had consumed that day and the pound I'm certain I gained from it. I was overwhelmed by fear they would weigh me, and the scale would reveal how big of a failure I was. To me, dying was better.

Interrupting the fear of weight gain were the sounds of sirens nearing the house. Pulling up to Grandma's house, I'm sure the neighbors worried it was my elderly grandparents. Who would've imagined all this fuss was for a teeny bopper risking her health and life for a few pounds? Who could've known this emergency was brought on by a child who didn't want to eat?

Looking back now through the lens of physical, mental, and emotional health, I just want to hold that frail child and tell her "It's going to be ok. You're going to be ok." And though I didn't feel the arms of my heavenly Father holding me, He was, and He was whispering, "It's going to be ok. You're going to be ok."

I don't remember the ambulance ride, but I do remember the hospital room. I was dehydrated and so the first thing they did was give me IV fluids. This panicked me more as I felt I would gain more weight with every drip of liquid going into my vein. I couldn't be sure this was just sodium and chloride. What if they were secretly giving me a weight gain supplement? I had lost all control. I couldn't even control what was running through my veins. I had lost the game. And I knew ED was going to be upset. I didn't know what I was afraid of more—my weight, my heart stopping, or ED's shame.

This incident scared my grandparents to death. They were aware of my disorder by name, but now they had seen its damaging effects—its control—over my life. And that was too much for them to bear. I was sent home to get help.

Chapter 3

Ready To Run

Back at home and more depressed and broken then when I had moved out the year before, I realized that living in a new state, with a new job and new friends only confirmed that the demons I was battling were inside me and not in the people or the geography. My parents, fearing for my life, admitted me to another hospital. This time it was to a specialized eating disorder clinic in Minneapolis, MN. It was there that I was ready to get help. I was exhausted, confused, and out of options. But through the darkness, I could see a tiny flickering light of hope.

Hope is a beautiful thing. Its debut only appears at the end of all odds. When you have nothing left, hope remains. Hope is the breath that keeps a person alive. And walking into the eating disorder clinic in Minneapolis, I clung to it.

No One Is Safe

Did you know that boys also suffer from eating disorders? Would it surprise you to learn that even at the tender age of 10, a boy could want to end his life and use an eating disorder as the means? It blew my mind to share a counseling room with these unlikely prisoners.

A 10-year-old boy sat across from me in a counseling session one day and I couldn't help but wonder what had happened in this boy's short life to be there with me. As I grappled with the idea that ED took this innocent boy captive before he was even in adolescence, I found motivation to beat this beast.

Befriending a shy, naive 14-year-old girl and promising her all her dreams would come true was almost justifiable but a 10-year-old! And if he was already seeking help, I wondered how old he was when ED groomed him. I was disgusted. I was appalled. I determined to beat him at his own game. Unfortunately, my tenacity was no match for my naivety. The force, influence, and power he had over me would keep me a prisoner for the next three decades.

What I didn't know at the time is that we are no contender for Satan. If he could be fully unleashed, he would ravage us. We would all end up on the sixth floor of the hospital. But in God's boundless love for us, He steps out of heaven and enters the battle on our behalf and in His great power always defeats the enemy. What we are living through is the futile attempt of Satan's short arm to grab us.

The week I was released was promising. I was healing. I was stronger. I decided to stay with my sister, Lauren, for a little while until I figured out what I wanted to do with my life. She had recently gotten married, so I would call her couch my home for a little while.

"Hey, would you like to start a workout regimen with me?" I asked my sister shortly after I moved in. I was determined to keep the momentum of health going. I knew if I made small achievable goals, I could reach them. And by doing so, I could reverse the damage ED had wreaked over my body, mind, and soul.

"You're the fat one! Get down and give me 20," she shot back.

Words as powerful as a gunshot wound to the heart hit my ears in disbelief. Ten careless, hateful, and bullying words from my sister were all it took to dismantle the three weeks of hard, emotionally exhausting work I had put in. The next day, I found myself bent over a toilet bowl flushing away my hope, my future, and my will to live. I wonder if the shrapnel hit my angel!

Hurt people hurt people. We've all heard it said. But I've always wondered how one who has had their heart stepped on and disrespected so badly could justify doing that to another. What reward or payoff does that person receive? I didn't stick around that day to find out. I refused to be anybody's payoff. And just like that, I was on the run again.

Running was my coping skill of choice. Whenever there was pain, hurt, anger, fear, or anxiety, I would run. Whether it was physical, emotional, or mental, the moment I smelled gunfire, I ran faster than the bullet could get to me. I became very good at detecting booby traps before detonating them. This was later diagnosed as PTSD in a counseling session three decades later.

Never had I contemplated fighting back.

Never would I respond with, "Why would you tell me that? You know I just got out of a mental hospital for an eating disorder! You have got to know that my weight is a hot topic that should be handled with care." No, those words would have to be backed up with strength, with confidence. I didn't possess any of those qualities.

I was only 18. My brain hadn't even been developed yet but sadly, I had already lived a life of regrets, secrets, and loneliness. I wanted to be someone else, anyone else. Gazing in the mirror at the empty shell of who I had become, I knew running was my best option. The idea of forging a new identity, one who wasn't weak, became my next quest. And an angel got a new pair of running shoes.

Heading Out West

I wanted to run but where could I go? With no friends or money, I challenged fate by opening a travel guide and pointing to an obscure location my finger gravitated toward. Red Willow Ranch, a dude ranch in Shoshone National forest on the east entrance road to Yellowstone National Park and 40 minutes west of Clear Water, WY. My family and I had vacationed a few years earlier at a nearby ranch and had enjoyed a week of horseback riding, white water rafting, hiking, and bonfires. So this seemed to be fate drawing me back in to what I once deemed as heaven, a place where I had forgotten my troubles—a place that wanted nothing in return.

Hesitantly I picked up the phone and dialed the number. "Hi, my name is Alora and I was wandering if you were hiring for summer help?"

I politely and shyly asked praying they were as if this was my only chance at saving my life.

"Well, you called at the perfect time. We were just going to post a help wanted ad," the owner responded with adventurous excitement to his voice.

Without much of an interview, I was offered a summer job. I would assist with making reservations, cleaning the cabins, and helping in the kitchen. This seemed like the perfect way to buy some time before having to make a more permanent life decision. So just as quickly as I was hired, I found myself packing up my car and heading out West. To help get me settled in, Mom and Dad trailed behind in their LTD Crown Victoria.

I loved my car, the first one I had ever owned. It was a cherry red 1984 Renault Encore hatchback. It was my ticket to freedom. With it, I could go wherever I wanted. The trip was eight hours long. As I drove on the flat pavement, sun beaming through the windows, I started to feel the effects of the monotonous landscape and hum of the engine. Exhausted and fighting the gravity of heavy eyelids, I found myself swerving toward the white line. Swerving back into my lane, I cracked down the window to get some fresh air on my face. Sitting up straight, I settled back in for another hour before the promised rest stop.

With a birds-eye view, my parents, trailing behind me, nervously watched as I swerved hugging the white line a little too close to their liking. We didn't have cell phones back then or else I'm sure they would've called me to tell me to pull over. So they just prayed and counted down the miles to the next rest area.

They had been married for 25 years and would soon be empty nesters. Getting me settled into my new home was the only thing left to do before officially having that title and enjoying the house to themselves. Though this would be an exciting stage for them in their relationship, I'm sure they questioned my choice to just pick up and live in a random place two states away. Had it been longer than a summer job, they might've had more questions for me. But they knew this wasn't forever and, in a way, it was like a summer vacation.

Finally, the rest area was a mile ahead. I knew I needed to get out and stretch my legs, hoping that would give me a burst of energy to carry me through the next few hours.

"I saw you swerving back there! What were you doing?" my mom questioned me, using a concerned tone.

"I was getting a little tired but I'm good now," responding casually, hoping this would satisfy her and put her at ease. I would soon find myself not so good.

"Okay, well get something to drink as well. We're only a few hours away," she said in her mom voice. Mom had a way of neutralizing the situation, or at least giving the impression her command would solve everything. This gave her peace of mind and I could continue living under the radar.

Chapter 4

Identity Crisis

I was 14 when ED and I met. He lured me in with promises of happiness, thinness, and numbness. It started off innocently—a diet here, a shake there, a little exercise to tone up, a missed meal to save a few calories. My mom was always dieting. Models in string bikinis plastered on magazine covers lined the supermarket aisles imploring us common folk that this was the key to happiness! ED offered me a secret life that promised beauty and love. All I had to do was obey him. My idol became thinness, and my god became ED.

Decades later I wrestled with the question of why I wanted to be numb in the first place. What had happened in 14 short years of a life to want to not feel anymore? How was it so easy to be manipulated by an ideology, a force? Could being thin really be all that I craved or was there more to that desire? I would later stumble upon the truth that my deepest desire was to fade away, to get so small I would not be visible. I literally wanted to disappear. But why? One does not wake up one day and say, "I want to destroy my life by being manipulated, abused, and controlled by an it." It promised me freedom. So why did I think I was a prisoner? Eventually, I would discover the answer to those questions but not before endless and reckless attempts at ending it all.

"Here it is! Red Willow Ranch." I said excitedly ready to start my new adventure. Here I could be whatever and whoever I wanted to be. "Hi, I'm Alora. I'm here for the job." I introduced myself eagerly.

"Welcome! Let me show you around and where you will be staying this summer," a man replied just as excited.

The owner was very kind. His face reflected the years of working on a ranch—sun-kissed lines filling in the creases of his smile. He reminded me of a gentle grandfather offering hope to a generation that was lost. Instantly I felt at home, or at least at a place where I could feel safe and free to be the new me.

I was given one day off a week. On those days, I could go wherever I wanted. I made friends quickly. When you're living with three or four other girls in the same room, it's easy to become buds. I was excited to go window shopping in Jackson Hole or walking around the geysers at Yellowstone National Park with my new friends. Unfortunately, we were a small staff and the lodge was never closed. So, we each got a different day off. We would have to do our exploring on our own, but in the evenings, we could hang out and get to know each other.

I lived life on the edge. Driving on winding, mountainous terrain, I would find myself going well above the speed limit and taking corners way too sharp. I'm certain the angels watching over me had to work overtime. I can imagine the angels picking straws to see who would have Alora duty. Or maybe they played rock, paper, scissors. I wander what would be easier for a guardian angel—watching out for someone who loved life or someone who questioned whether death would be better?

I was 18 and felt invincible. Or maybe it was I just didn't care what happened to me. Maybe it was a deeper craving of wanting to see just how far I could push the envelope, while leaving fate in someone else's hands.

I grew up learning all about God and His Son, Jesus, but I didn't know Him personally. I didn't know of the relationship we could have with the triune God. It was all rules and nothing more. In fact, I was certain God didn't care what I did, as long as I looked good on the outside and didn't embarrass my parents. He had way too many other important people to care about and not me, a teeny bopper who was ashamed of wearing the 'I love Jesus' t-shirts my grandmother would send me. Or the girl who purged in the church bathroom, hoping being this close to God would either strike me dead or resurrect my already dead soul. If God was something other than a moral code to live by, I sure didn't act like it.

And when I moved to Wyoming, I left my Christianity at home. I was done being the shy, insecure, pastor's kid who was never invited to parties. I was through with my yearly best friend trading me in for someone much cooler. I was ready to try on a new identity.

After working all day on the ranch, my new friends and I would drive down to the neighboring ranches and hang out until all hours of the night drinking and partying. The ranch bars didn't care how old you were. If you had money, you were leaving with product. Quickly I became a regular, buying for my friends and hoping this lifestyle would bring me happiness. I was soaking in hot tubs with strangers, making out with nameless guys, and cursing like it was my native tongue. The person I was becoming looked nothing like the person who arrived just a few short weeks earlier. But soon my momentary facade would come face to face with something greater than myself.

Sitting at the campfire one night, we shared stories of our families—where we came from and where we were headed. I sat and listened soaking up the laughter and imagining trading places with one of them. What would it look like to have a family who cared, a family who loved me unconditionally? The last four years of my life had been a blur. I had been taken captive by an elusive force in my own home so innocuous that my captured soul mirrored a normal withdrawn teenager counting down the days until she could spread her wings and fly. I wondered if my friends' parents would've been able to tell the difference between the two.

Intoxicated

Drinking was my fast track to living out my new identity. It lowered my inhibitions and dissolved any trace of the girl back home. I loved this reckless, wild spirit that came out when I drank too much. She was fun! She was brave! She was everything the real me wasn't. I thought if I was her more than I was me then eventually it would no longer be a façade. I would just morph into this new person and the lies and deception would turn to truth. The boys liked this girl. The girls would never think to trade her in for someone cooler. She had become the cool kid.

This wasn't the first time I drank. In fact, by the time I was sitting around a campfire in Wyoming, I had had my fair share of underage drinking. My first drink and second and seventh were in my sister's apartment at one of her parties. That inconspicuous night would prove to leave its mark. No one could have suspected that this party would forever change the lives of so many people.

I found an instant attraction to alcohol. It had become my plus one. I didn't have to worry about being awkward or shy. I was perfectly fine dancing the night away with my friends and my intoxication. My best friend, Lucy, however, found an instant attraction to one of my sister's friends. He was in the Air Force and much older than she was. He swooped in and swept her off her feet. They started seeing each other after that night and after a while Lucy found out she was pregnant. At just 17 years old, her life was changed forever. She hoped for a fairytale ending she was promised as a child of living happily ever after. Unfortunately for her, this childhood fantasy gave way to an adult reality. She would end up carrying a child throughout her senior year of high school and giving birth at the young age of 18.

As my life continued with parties and irresponsibility, her life changed to motherhood. No longer would she be my drinking buddy and dance partner. Instead, she would be nursing an infant, changing diapers, and becoming sleep deprived while trying to figure out how to do it alone. Her boyfriend hightailed it out of the relationship and out of their lives. Fortunately, her family stepped up and helped raise Alex. He became her pride and joy. However, our friendship was never the same. I moved away and like the saying goes, "out of sight, out of mind."

And my sister, Lauren? While I was passed out in the bathtub, she was flirting with an airman. Standing 6'1" tall, Sam was different than any of the other men my sister had gone out with. He was reserved, shy, and just what my sister was looking for. She loved the way he spoke softly and made her feel like she was the only one in the room. She instantly felt an attraction to him and that night they started dating.

The Bible teaches us that God is omnipresent, which means He's everywhere, and not everywhere at a specific moment in time but in the past and in the future. As I reflect on that night when I was passed out in the bathtub, I wonder what God thought of me. I imagine He looked on me with grave concern. He wasn't worried what would happen to me because He knew, but rather He grieved for how much joy and peace I was forfeiting by choosing this lifestyle.

If you received a snapshot of how your relationships would end prior to jumping in with both feet and that picture would reveal the pain, betrayal, and hurt accompanying that investment, would you want to peek? If you did, would you decide it's not worth it and walk away? What if a beautiful daughter came out of that relationship? Would you still walk away? Every byproduct of the choices we make will ultimately end up being the thing that moves us toward or away from God.

Lauren ended up marrying Sam, and pain, betrayal, and hurt followed soon after. But so did Carly, a beautiful brown-eyed, dark wavy-haired, little girl whose smile could melt your heart. Lauren remained in an abusive relationship for a decade before finally getting the courage to walk or should I say run away. And from that relationship she found herself running into the arms of another prince who would later reveal his true self. The price we pay for love, acceptance, and a chance at happiness is more than Christ will ever demand from us, and He is the real deal. He will deliver on every promise He makes to His children.

Alcohol was the price I paid to be someone else. A substance without regret had as much control and power over me as ED himself. I found myself in a tug of war for control between alcohol and ED. The lost girl trying to find love and happiness had been taken hostage by two incredibly powerful forces. I was no longer recognizable. The worst part was I liked the battle for my soul. At least someone or in this case something was fighting for me. To them, I was important, and it felt good to be wanted. If God was lurking in the shadows or holding me, I didn't notice.

Chapter 5

Sibling Rivalry

"It's my turn," my older sister, Diane yelled as she grabbed my hair and pulled me off the piano bench. This was a story Lauren would tell me decades later. I have no memory of my childhood abuse except for a slap across my face at 17. However, both my sister who abused me and my other sister confirmed it did happen.

I've wrestled with God on so many occasions to help me open my memory box and let me see what happened to me, but He gently declines my requests, pleads, and silent treatments. One time I literally screamed at Him, "They're my memories! You have no right to keep them from me!!" I continued, "I need to know what happened to me. Why won't you just let me see? I'm grown up now. I can handle it."

Emotionally spent I would sob like a teenage girl being told she couldn't go to the school dance. But I would always come back to believing God, who in His great compassion and mercy for me, chose to spare me the visual depiction of the emotional pain I experienced.

Diane was five years older than I and a lot bigger. She struggled in school due to a learning disability, which caused delayed development both academically and socially. She was insecure and paranoid that everyone was watching her. She wouldn't even go out to eat for fear that people would stare, causing her high anxiety. All this insecurity and inner turmoil threw her into fits of rage that was most often directed at me. At times, I don't even think it was Diane.

Diane had her own demons. And from the time I was born, I became the object of her wrath. Whether it was slapping me or embarrassing me, she had become my real life, under-the-bed boogie man. She even chased me in my dreams. But not understanding the world outside my window and what was acceptable, I learned to accept this as normal sibling rivalry and nothing out of the ordinary. All sisters fight or at least I made myself believe that. Anytime I tried to tell my parents what she was doing, it was met with, "That's just Diane. Just try to get along."

Growing up in this kind of environment taught me how to survive early on. I learned how to walk on eggshells to avoid waking the giant. I began to recognize what I would call "rumblings" that gave me a little bit of time to prepare myself for the earthquake. These rumblings were little changes in her tone, word choice, body language, or her passive aggressiveness. Upon hearing and seeing these, I would take cover.

I prepared an exit strategy in my mind which was to be faster than she was. Being a scrawny seven-year--old third grader could not compete with a middle-school bully. So, I learned to run and hide. I never grew the confidence to fight back but I learned the magic trick of disappearing. When I got to be older, I kept running and trying to disappear by using other measures. My real-life boogie man continued attacking me throughout my life. And my parents? To them, she was the victim. She was the one who needed help. She was the one they loved, they fought for, they cared about.

As I found myself back in counseling years later to heal from my past, I reached out to my sister in a desperate quest to learn all I could about my past. "What did you do to me?" I implored my sister to answer. "Why can't I remember anything from my past?" I desperately pleaded with her to fill in the blanks.

And then a story she had kept hidden for decades came spewing out her mouth. "I saved you!" she said in an almost exasperated way. She continued, "When you were an infant, our babysitter's boyfriend came over and raped me. He told me that if I said anything to anyone about what he did, he would come back and kill you. So, by keeping it a secret all this time, I saved you." She ended as if she should win the sister-of-the-year award.

"So, tell me how abusing me saved me?" I asked, utterly confused.

"You were the reason I couldn't tell anyone about the rape," she said as if it all made sense now. "And because I couldn't tell anyone, it ate me up. When I couldn't take the pain of it anymore, my anger would explode from me. Since you were the reason I couldn't say anything, I grew to hate you. Does that make sense?" she replied.

"To make matters worse, I truly believed Dad loved you more than me," she continued, unburdening herself while stacking the blocks onto me. "I needed someone to love me enough to notice my pain and seeing you get all the attention just made you my enemy. But I love you so much and I'm so sorry," she said, hoping this would make up for the 40 years of trauma.

Hanging up the phone, my head was spinning. Part of me didn't believe her. Repeatedly she would coax me into believing she was never responsible for things that I know she deliberately did to sabotage me. There was the time she stole my keys off my desk at work and left me stranded. Or the time she called my work pretending like an upset customer I waited on to get me fired. She was a master manipulator, and I was her prey. My counselor would later diagnose her as a gas-lighter with a multi-personality disorder. She knew how to push my buttons and how to tug on my heart strings to highlight her as the victim.

But thinking about it further, I realized it kind of made sense. If I in fact was the reason she had to keep this abuse a secret for my protection, I could see how she could grow to hate me. I was the obstacle to her seeking help. And just like that, I found myself once again in an emotional web of confusion. What's truth, what's false, and who's safe?

At that point I knew I wasn't going to get the answers I was looking for from my abuser and thus get my memories back. So, I reconciled that I didn't need to know what happened in the past to heal from my past. But what I did come to believe was I couldn't move beyond my past if the people who hurt me the most were in my present. I made the decision to cut all ties with both my sisters. Sibling rivalry had been mislabeled for what was taking place and if no one was going to advocate for me, then I needed to do it for myself.

Chapter 6

The Crash

"Hey, who wants my wine coolers?" I soberly asked.

It wasn't like me not to participate in an evening of getting wasted around a campfire. But something in me was pulling me towards sobriety. Was it responsibility? I knew I had to wake up at 4 a.m. to take my friend to the airport. But that never crossed my mind. Was it generosity? Though I did crave being liked and knew giving people things made me more likeable, they were all stocked with their drink of choice. Nothing made sense for me to give up the thing that had given so much life to me. But I had this pull, this desire to not drink. So, I didn't.

I called it a night at 2 a.m. knowing I would only get two hours of sleep. Before settling in for the night, I got two of my friends to commit to going with me to take our friend to the airport. "Good night. I'll wake you up in two hours" were the last words spoken before falling off into a peaceful rest.

"Time to get up girls!" I said, softly yawning under the words.

"No, I'm too tired," one of the committed friends responded.

"How about you, girl?" I pleaded with my other friend.

"I'm still so wasted. You're on your own!" Her words biting back not realizing how true they were to me. And off we were to make the 40-minute drive to Clear Water, Wyoming.

Dark and winding roads, almost instigating a challenge, stared back at me as I struggled to keep my eyelids open. Memories of this same feeling just a few months earlier brought a sense of dread. Would I not be as lucky as last time? I almost felt like death came to warn me. It was eerie yet expected. I did only get two hours of sleep. I just needed to roll down my window like before.

"Man, I'm sleepy. How are you doing?" my friend asked almost like she was reading my mind.

"I'm good," I said inconspicuously.

"Well, I'd get some coffee before you head back. I'd hate for you to fall asleep at the wheel," she responded like she knew what lied ahead.

I wish I drank coffee, but I couldn't stand the taste or smell of it. I thought about the summer road trips we'd take to Grandma's house. Hopping into the pea green Buick, we'd pick up where we left off with the license plate game. We tried to find as many out-of-state plates as we could. When that got boring, we would play the alphabet game with road signs. As we got older, the games were replaced with magazines and Walkmans.

I remember the smell of coffee permeating the cabin of the car for the entire trip. Dad would fill up his thermos right before we hit the road. By the time we got to a rest area, he would need to fill up again. He could drink a pot of coffee before mid-day and still have a craving for it later in the evening. The smell of black Folger's coffee mixed with the sound of talk radio was almost too much to bear. It was the cost of going to Grandma's house. And even when I was barely able to keep myself awake for the trip back to the ranch, I refused to drink coffee. I was invincible, right?

I said my goodbyes and promised I'd stay in touch. I was no stranger to farewells. I had already moved eight times, and I viewed friends as chapters in my life. Though I promised I'd stay in touch, it was more of a desire, a hope. But deep down I knew friends came and went in my life. Not that I meant to, but I handled friendships like paper plates instead of fine china—they became disposable. Stretching my legs and grabbing some water, I headed back for the ranch.

By now the sun was starting to peak over the Rocky Mountains through a blanket of lazy clouds. Still fighting to stay awake, I turned up my music and sat back up in my chair. Cranking up the air and aiming the vents to slap me in the face, I took a sip of water. I was just about ten minutes away from climbing back into my bunk, getting under my covers, and finishing up my night's sleep.

What's that noise? I couldn't place the sound. It was getting louder and closer. Realizing my eyes were closed I quickly shot them back open. I was met with a telephone pole staring back at me, like it was challenging me to make the first move. There wasn't time to make a calculated decision. I didn't have the opportunity to ask myself if I should slam on the brakes or swerve to miss it. And if I chose to swerve, should I turn to the left or to the right? I had to make a split-second decision. Instinctively I must've known that the stopping time would exceed the space between the pole and my car. So, I chose to swerve to the left.

Was I flying? Had I been stopped mid-air? Did time freeze, like the space in between jumping off a diving board and contacting the water below? Quiet, peaceful, held—that is all I felt. What was happening? I couldn't hear anything. I couldn't see anything. Then as if I was gently placed on display, I found myself underwater, hanging upside down.

I began pleading with God to rescue me. Isn't that what we do when we realize we are so much smaller than we think we are, when we conclude we're not invincible? Would the God I left at home be willing to rescue me now? Would He be willing to save me even though I did everything possible to kick him out of my life that summer? Would my life even be worth redeeming?

Calling My Bluff

As I pleaded with God to save me, I reflected on the irony of trying to end it all just a year earlier when I was at Grandma's house, fighting depression and ED. In my room one day, I began a conversation with myself. "Who would care anyway? Who would miss me?" I rolled over on my bed and came face to face with my pill bottle. I had been taking some anti-depressants that year hoping they would bring me out of the pit I found myself in—as if a small blue pill was a magic bullet. Was it fate that our eyes met? Was it poetic that the pill promising to bring me up could take me under? I flirted with the idea of taking them all and just falling asleep, never to wake up again. No more pain, no more striving. I was one decision away from those questions being answered.

I walked over to the bottle and just stared at it, expecting it to reprimand me for just the thought of using them for anything other than what they were meant for. I was alone but for a moment I hoped someone would barge in and spoil my plan. I needed someone to tell me, "You matter, you're worthy. You don't need to prove a thing." But no one came in.

Slowly I began to twist off the cap. Pouring the small happy pills into my palm, I gazed down at my hand and took a deep breath. Here goes everything, I said with mixed emotions. Popping them all into my mouth and chugging down a glass of water, there was no turning back. I thought to myself, *How could I be so sure I wanted to end my life? So sure, there was no one who loved me the way I needed them to. Would the God I grew numb to actually be willing to intervene and breathe new life into my lifeless soul?*

Our brains are so complex and what they do with our memories is almost criminal. They can recognize the moments that bring us so much pain and with seeming compassion take them into hiding, never to be relived again—even as memories. That's how the memory of the night I overdosed on my medication became another victim to memory suppression.

So why did I care about my life now? As I begged God to save my petty life, I wondered why today was different. If God chose not to save me, that would secure my true desire of disappearing, right? What more could I ask for? I was getting what I longed for—to float away into oblivion.

Closing my eyes and conceding to death was the last thing I remember before breaking the river's ceiling. I was alive! Being dragged by the water's current, I clung to my leather jacket that had somehow been ripped off during the rescue. Suddenly my chest made contact with a small island in the middle of the riverbed filled with rocks and washed me onto shore. The sun was still trying to peak through the newly awakened clouds, but bright enough to reveal the evidence of what just happened. Grasping the enormity of the situation, I screamed for my mommy who was two states away. Then remembering who just saved me, I cried out to God, thanking Him for still caring for me. Immediately I started telling Him what I was going to do—go back to church and return to Him.

The mist from sleepy clouds fighting to wake up filled the air. Looking around and spotting the mountainside, I realized I had fallen at least 30 feet and was at the bottom of a cliff. No one would spot me down there. I knew I had to get back into the water to cross over to the edge. This wasn't a tourist's entrance to the river where you could fly fish or sunbathe on the water's edge. I reconciled that the only way back up was the way I had come down.

I wasn't hurt. The thought to check myself out didn't even occur to me. I was alive but did anything break in the process? If it had, I was unaware of it both physically and mentally. All I could concentrate on was climbing up the steep embankment to the main road and flagging someone down. So, going back into the cold water that once threatened to take my life, I began to swim to the edge. I don't remember the current being as strong. It was like God told the waters to be still.

Climbing up the side of the cliff, I determined that my life had been reset. I was given a second chance and I had better take it seriously. Soaking wet from head to toe, I took one step at a time climbing up the steep cliff. I had been knocked down so many times prior to this day and somehow, I managed to keep taking another step. I imagine God was whispering into my soul, "You matter, keep climbing!"

Arriving at the top, I planted my feet on pavement and began waving down an RV slowly approaching my location. I can just imagine the conversation inside that RV. "What on earth is that up ahead? Is that a girl?" Slowly pulling over to the side, I ran across the street to meet up with them. They were an older couple probably on their way to a nearby ranch for the weekend. As our eyes met, a rolled-up window in between us, I said with my voice cracking, "Hi. Can you help me?"

The lady just sat there shaking her head no. What about me scared them so much that they were unwilling to help me? Were they driving across country to visit their little grandchildren who they hadn't seen in months and I had delayed their plans? Then why did they even stop? I couldn't believe she was unwilling to help another human being who was obviously in need of help. There I was, a child looking like a drowned rat asking for help and this grown-up was unwilling. Maybe from her perspective she thought it was all a ruse. As soon as she would roll down her window, my accomplice would jump out of the bushes and attack her? To me the idea was ludicrous, but maybe she had her reasons. Either way, God interceded and made a way to help me.

Angel In Disguise

"I'll take you where you need to go," the smiling young traveler said who had just appeared out of nowhere. Draping a blanket over my shoulders, he led me to his truck. Unclear just how far away the camp was, I settled in and began to soak up the hot air being spewed out of the vents. Conversation was minimal, as if what just happened was already known to him. Before I knew it, he was pulling to my camp. The crash site was just ten short miles away.

"Are you going to be ok?" the gentleman asked, as I jumped out and thanked him for the ride.

"I will be," I said unsure what the fuss was all about. I slowly made my way to the barracks I was staying in. Still dripping wet from being submerged, I got two feet in the door when my friends frantically asked what happened.

"Oh, I was just in a car accident, but I'm totally fine." I casually replied as if they would respond in like. I was exhausted and cold. I just wanted to change and get back under my blanket and drift back to sleep. Adrenaline had been pumping through my body masking any pain I had but I didn't realize it.

"Call an ambulance!" my friend screamed to the other. Leading me slowly out of the cabin to the main entrance, they saw our boss who was getting things set up for the day.

"What happened?" the owner shrieked, uncertain how serious it was.

"She was in a car accident and I think she's in shock. The ambulance is on their way." My friend was a take-charge kind of girl. She must've been raised by brothers having to live up to the family standard or maybe she was from a large family where she needed to find her voice early in life if she would ever be listened to. Somehow at 18 she knew what to do. We sat in the restaurant's bar waiting for the ambulance to arrive. I still didn't understand what all the fuss was about. I was fine.

Chapter 7

Daddy's Girl

"Ann, wake up!" my father screamed being catapulted from his sleep. "Something has happened to Alora. I don't know what, but something has happened!"

These were the words I would later hear from my dad's perspective of the accident. What kind of behind the scenes, front-row view had my father been privileged to witness as he lay in a deep sleep? What was God's intent to startle my father the way He did? God knew I was fine. Why did he feel the need to disturb a resting man two states away who couldn't do anything for me anyway? Within minutes from being abruptly awakened, the phone rang. It was a Clear Water police officer who was given this case.

"Is this James Franklin Walker?" the cop asked, sounding very official.

"Yes, is my daughter Alora okay?" my father replied with a crack in his voice now aware this could be the call that brought conclusions to his premonition.

My father used to be a police officer in

Dallas, Texas where he was assigned one of the roughest beats in downtown Dallas. He had a K-9 and a gun, and he used them both on many nights. He knew the sound of official business. And coupled with my father's nightmare, he knew something wasn't right.

My father and I had a very complicated relationship, at least from my perspective. The complication lied in the fact that his love for me lacked connection or action. This became a common thread in my family. Words like love, sorry, and family lost its meaning after a while. When words are not backed up by action, or worse yet are opposite to its definition, it weakens their power. And when all you have in a relationship are words lacking action, you just have a void. And that was the definition of my relationship with my dad—a void.

Knowledge is a weird thing. Sometimes it's just there. You don't have a memory of when you collided with it. Often, I will think about something and wonder how in the world do I not remember this transference of information. For instance, my name or better yet why I was named Alora.

My parents waited until I was born to name me. I'm sure they were thinking about the perfect name that would suit me but wanted to see if it would match my face. My mother worked with a lady at a title company whose name was Alora. So, the day she was in labor, she floated that name by my dad. He loved it and just like that they had a name ready for me when I arrived.

My mom told me that when she went into

labor with me it only took three pushes, and I was out. I guess by the time you have a third child muscles aren't as strong down there as they used to be! Swaddled and held in mother's arms, I was just as content as in the womb. I'm not sure how long they celebrated the birth of their third child before my father let my mom know the real reason he liked my name. But I know it had been enough time for the ink to dry on the birth certificate.

Marriage Masquerade

"Ann, I have to tell you something," my father said, hoping the excitement of a newborn would overshadow any bad news she was about to hear.

"Yes, dear, what is it?" my mother replied half listening to dad and half listening to the sounds of newborn breaths.

"The real reason I said I liked the name Alora is because there's a lady I know who is named Alora. There's nothing going on between us, but I wanted to let you know just in case you meet her and wonder if that's the reason," my father said, apologizing for her own assumption.

In the years to follow, my father would struggle with infatuation for other women. He never acted on those feelings but on more than one occasion he found himself wanting to be the hero for those other women. I don't know when I was told I was named after a lady in my father's fantasy world, but I do know the effects of that confession sabotaged the first year of my mother being able to bond with me. This news sent her into a depression and set me up for emotional neglect.

They say the bond between a mother and a daughter in the first year of life is crucial to their physical and emotional development. Due to emotionally absentee parents, I developed a detachment disorder I would discover decades later. I found myself wanting to get close to anyone who had a strong parental aura about them. I lacked a sense of security and nurture. Ironically, I developed my own type of infatuation with people. I began dreaming what it would be like to have that person as my dad or that lady as my mom. Even as an adult I would find myself just wanting to be held in a lap of someone who I felt would be safe.

Dad had a nickname for all his kids and mine was Alora Bean. It was endearing, almost making up for the first year of my life that my mother was living in bitterness. But some things are just too heavy to balance out the scales.

I wish I could say my father realized how great he had it with a beautiful wife, three healthy daughters, a career in law enforcement, and the respect of one who had served his country. But he battled discontentment. And when I was three years old, my mother gave him an ultimatum.

"I'm moving back home and I'm taking the girls with me. You can come with me or not. I don't care," my mother boldly proclaimed, trying to be strong for everyone.

Home was California and we were still in Dallas. Mother just couldn't take the lies, empty promises, and split loyalties any longer. If he wanted to remain married, he would have to quit his job, cease his emotional infidelities, and put the family's needs first. To his credit, he put in for a transfer and moved with the family to California.

Their relationship didn't start off like most. My father had been dating my mother's sister, Maggie, when he was in the service. My mother would tell me that every night she would go into Maggie's room and stare at the picture of Dad on her dresser. She said he was the most handsome man she had ever seen. Dark hair, blue eyes, and just shy of 6 feet, my dad was striking. And my mother had a thing for men in uniform. She would daydream about James being her boyfriend and him coming home from war and picking her up off her feet and spinning her around. They would kiss and sparks would fly. Then one day fantasy morphed into reality.

Maggie was a wild child. She was always different and spoke her mind. She knew what she wanted and went after it. However, she wanted more than what she could have—two men. While Dad was off fighting battles, Maggie had been cheating on him with another man. She decided to break up with him. My mom's other sister, Suzanne, knew Mom had a thing for James so shortly after the break-up Suzanne threw a party and invited both James and Mom and became a match-maker. And just like that, Mom and Dad began dating.

Mom couldn't believe that a handsome serviceman would ever like her, much less want to marry her. But after a few short weeks of dating, Dad proposed. They wanted to get married before he had to go overseas so they decided to get married a few months later. But with any whirlwind romance novel, there is always a plot twist that threatens the relationship, and Mom and Dad's story was no different.

A letter arrived in the mail the morning of their wedding with no return address on the envelope. Mom opened it and read words that pierced her heart: 'He's in love with me, not you. He will never love you the way he loves me.'

"The wedding is off, James!" my mother yelled, running out the back door.

"What are you talking about?" my father replied as he chased her down, dazed and confused.

Throwing the letter in his face, she said, "I got a letter from your girlfriend saying you love her! What is this? Who is this?" My mother was inconsolable.

"Ann, I love you. She's some crazy girl I dated for a blink of an eye. Can't you see she's just trying to ruin what we have?" Dad said, pleading with her.

Realizing his love for her was stronger than what she had come to know, she reconsidered and walked down the aisle saying 'I do' and praying she was doing the right thing. But just as they were enjoying their first meal together as a married couple, she caught dad checking out the waitress. *What did I get myself into?* my mom sighed as the waitress walked by.

Twenty-seven years later, they were still together. And this day, they would find themselves traveling two states to rescue me. Jumping into their car, my mother and father headed out for Red Willow Ranch.

Chapter 8

The Miracle

Running in with a spinal board, the medics wrapped me up like a mummy. They had seen firsthand what car accidents can do to the body, especially on the inside, and were not willing to take any chances. All I could see after that were the ceiling tiles. As they carted me off to the ambulance, I began counting them one by one. I was still in shock, unable to comprehend what had just happened. I was exhausted by then and just wanted to sleep, but they weren't about to let me do that.

As they lifted me into the ambulance, I remembered my last time I had been in one of those just a year earlier. Things had sure changed since that last ride. I was in a different state, living in different conditions, and with different fears. That day I had peace. A few hours earlier I might've had similar fears, but my resurrected body found a calmness in what my friends called an emergency. Driving east toward Clear Water, I wondered if it was more difficult for God to save a starving girl or a rebellious one.

"Ouch! It hurts so bad," I told the radiologist who was taking my x-rays.

By now my body had awakened from its two-hour shock slumber. Every turn, every pull was met with excruciating pain. My mind and body were finally reunited, and I realized my accident had left me pretty banged up.

"I'm sorry, but it's important we get full body x-rays. You were in a pretty serious car accident," she responded as if I should've been expecting the pain.

"Why didn't I feel the pain right after the accident?" I asked expecting anyone in a white coat to be able to answer all medical questions.

"Your body went into shock and the adrenaline released from that masked the underlying pain you are still experiencing. You're coming out of shock now and so the pain is being unmasked," she said, explaining what seemed obvious.

I was sent back to my room to await the results of my tests. Just then a police officer entered my room and began to question me.

"Are you Alora Walker?" he asked in an official tone.

"I am," I replied, not expecting a police officer to show up at the hospital.

"I wanted to ask you some questions about the accident you were involved in. Is that okay?" He asked as if he would just turn back around and walk out if I said no.

"You went off the cliff going westbound on Hwy 14, is that right?" he started.

"I guess. I just know I was headed back to Red Willow Ranch from Clear Water when I fell asleep at the wheel and swerved to miss a pole. I guess that's westbound on Hwy 14. I'm not that good with directions," I nervously replied, hoping I answered according to how I should have.

"And tell me, were you alone at the time of the accident?" he continued his interrogation.

"Yes sir," responding confidently to an answer I knew.

"Since you were alone and didn't damage any property, I won't cite you. But please be careful and don't drive when you haven't gotten enough sleep." He sounded like he was scolding a child to try and scare them into responsibility.

I know it was his job to get the facts of what happened, but I just wanted to sleep.

"Thank you, officer. Did you get in touch with my parents?" I asked, half hoping they would walk in even as we spoke.

"I did and they're on their way," he responded as he left my room.

Relieved that their love crossed state lines, I imagined them running into the camp, throwing their arms around my neck, and asking me if I was okay. As I pondered telling them about my crash, I wondered how much would I have to tell them about my new identity? Did I need to include the parties I attended or the boys I made out with? How about the second language I learned so quickly? Or the fact that at times an underwater burial sounded perfect? Could my spiritual wake-up call be explained shy of those details?

The doctor entered my room with a look of amazement on her face. "Well, the x-ray reveals you're perfectly fine! No broken bones or internal bleeding." Not believing what she was saying since she knew the details of my accident, she concluded, "Someone was sure looking out for you." Then she turned and walked away.

Part of me was not shocked. I knew God had saved me in the waters that morning. I figured if He was going to go to all that trouble rescuing me, He may as well get some attention. And boy, my miracle did indeed point to God's power.

At that point, I was feeling much better. The doctor had given me some pain medicine, along with a prescription to use as needed, and that was that. I had escaped a near-death accident. I concluded God threw me off a cliff to get my attention. To wake me up. To get me to stop running. To turn back to him. And that is what I did.

The hospital called my boss to tell them I had been released and to send someone to pick me up. My boss dutifully sent one of the staff members to bring me home. As irony would have it, the boy had a two-seater truck with no working seatbelts. It was kind of eerie getting back into a vehicle, much less one that wouldn't secure me fully. But at the same time, I remembered how the seat belt had trapped me under the water as well. So off we went back to the lodge. I don't remember the ride back but I'm sure driving past the accident site would've caused my heart to sink.

The next day my parents arrived at the camp. We hugged and exchanged pleasantries. I showed them the laceration on my neck and the multiple bruises that covered my legs. I couldn't help but wonder how those bruises got there since I was held throughout the entire fall. And even crashing into the river, I never felt like I moved. I had never felt more protected by God than when He was holding me. This supernatural experience shifted my entire purpose, existence, and priorities.

The Wreckage

Years after the accident, I would have dreams of falling off the cliff and experiencing the same peace and grip I felt as I was descending. I would wake up and hope this version of the dream would uncover another detail of the crash, but it never did. All I knew was God saved me again that day and I would live my life in gratitude to Him.

My parents and I went to the junkyard that afternoon. By then, my car had been hoisted out of the river and taken to a vehicle cemetery. Walking past other beat-up cars and trucks, I spotted my little red Renault Encore. Sitting next to a van, it looked a lot smaller than it had the day before.

I remember the day I got my first car. I was 16 years old and ready to gain freedom. Though my school was three blocks away, I would drive there. I also enjoyed going into town with a few friends on the weekends and cruising up and down Main Street, looking for cute boys to hang out with. But now it sat in a car cemetery never to bring excitement to a teenager again.

"Oh my gosh, Alora! How did you walk away from that?" Mom said in disbelief.

Staring at the caved in roof, the engine that hung on by a wire, inverted tires, and a crushed hatch, I felt disbelief as well. This was now part of my story. The God of the universe has spared my life for a reason, a purpose. I felt revived that day looking at a vehicle that wouldn't have the same conclusion. Its time as a car was over. It would soon be crushed and recycled to be used as something else. And in a way, that was true of myself. I had been crushed. I had been lifted out of the water. And I was going to be used for another purpose.

Chapter 9

Recycled

I left the next day with my mom and dad to return to North Dakota. I left a different person. No longer was I the re-invented reckless girl who partied to get noticed. Nor was I the girl who wanted to re-invent herself in the first place. That day I had a reunion with the girl that I had only seen glimpses of throughout my life. A girl who resembled the reflection I saw when being held by my grandmother. A girl who was content with life not being fair. A girl who had been recycled for a greater purpose.

Realizing I was that girl mostly in the presence of my grandma, Ingrid, I knew I needed to move back to California. By now, my grandma had heard the miracle story of my crash. But no one knew the miracle that was happening in my heart. I didn't even know it. I felt a change, a shift, but I had no idea what that meant in the grand scheme of things. I clung to my list of good verses and knew I needed to clean up my act. No more cussing, drinking, or boys. But rather, church, friends, and family.

"Hi Grandma, this is Alora." I said, having no idea how this conversation would go.

"Oh Alora. I heard all about your car accident. How are you doing?" she said, in her warm, loving voice.

"It was a miracle, Grandma. I didn't even break a bone!" I replied, still so very thankful to God for rescuing me.

"God is so very good to us. Are you sore at all?" Grandma continued in her nurturing way.

"A little. But mostly I'm just grateful to be alive so much so that the pain doesn't bother me. I really can't believe God helped me. I was so terrible to Him," I said, knowing that I could tell Grandma anything without feeling judged.

"So, what are you going to do now?" she inquired.

The moment came. I was standing at a T in the road and her response to my request would determine the direction of my life. I was nervous. I had already been there just a year prior and had put both my grandparents through so much. I told myself that if she didn't let me move back in with them, that I would be okay. That would not reflect her lack of love for me but rather just a hardship for her to take on.

"I was thinking I could try living with you and Grandpa again. I'm a lot better now with my eating and knowing God saved me from my accident. I have much to prove," I said, as if I were responding to a parole board.

"Would you look for a job while you're here?" Grandma asked, somewhat intrigued by the idea I wanted to try this again.

"Most definitely. I was thinking of getting a job as a nanny. I hear there are a lot of opportunities for nanny jobs in California," I replied, getting excited even as I spoke.

"That's a great idea. Let me talk with Grandpa about this. I know it didn't work out before, but I know you have done a lot of work in getting help. I'm sure he'll be fine with it. I'll let you know what we decide in a few days," she said in a hopeful tone.

"Thank you, Grandma. I love you so much," I said, as tears welled up in my eyes.

Tilting my head back to hold the tears in its place, I prayed to God. "God, I know You have a better life for me than the one I tried to make for myself. I know You love me and no matter what Grandma decides, I trust You will provide for me."

As I Lay Me Down To Sleep

I used to pray a lot. There were times all I could do to get through the day was to reach up to God and in simplicity ask Him to let me know He was there. Remembering those times and by now seeing the results of His presence, I began to smile and have peace. I rationalized that if He saved me, He must have an awesome plan for me, and I would just have to have patience. After what I put my family through and turning my back on God, patience was the least I could give.

Prayer has since become a lifeline for me. Whether I'm wading through self-inflicted pain or pain heaped on me because of other's decisions, I have always known I have an anchor in Christ that will never be moved. I will always have the assurance that God is working on my behalf. He is so good, and His mercy and grace have never run out on me. He has even proven, not that He ever had to, that regardless of me unhooking myself from this anchor, He continued to follow me, love me, protect me, and hold me.

"Hi Alora, this is Grandma," Ingrid said in a tone that got my hopes up.

"Hi Grandma. How are you?" I asked, as if just shooting the breeze and not dying to know her answer.

"Well, Grandpa and I talked and decided that we'd love to have you come back and stay with us. Are you still wanting that?" she responded, in such a way that unearthed my tears from days prior.

"Grandma, you won't be sorry. I'm so happy, and I'm so grateful." I said in between sniffles.

"I'm so happy that you want to stay with us. It means a lot," she said. And just like that, the trajectory of my life was set in motion.

As I reflect on that day from her perspective, I wonder if she ever felt regret for sending me away in the darkest moments of my life. Even if she believed this was for the best for me, there had to be moments of uncertainty. Would I blame her? Would this jeopardize our closeness? Her response to me that she was happy I wanted to come back might have been tinged with relief. But to me, it was grace!

It had been just two short weeks since my car accident, but I was ready. I was anticipating great things. I knew I had been given a second chance not only at life but with Grandma and

Grandpa and I wasn't going to blow it. I set out on a mission, a mission to not disappoint. It was a mission to find out who the real Alora was. It was a mission that would require a lot of time, friends, and more of God's grace.

Chapter 10

New Kid On The Block

My grandparents attended First Baptist Church in Santa Elia, so I started attending with them. At first, I only went to the church service with them, wanting to stay right by their side. I was used to being a small fish in a small pond. Now I was living in a town that was bigger than the last three places I had lived in combined. I found myself battling the desire to want to disappear as well as the drive to start living. I knew every decision I made would be analyzed to make sure I wouldn't fall back into old patterns.

In that first month, I said yes to social invitations more often than I was comfortable with just to pacify any concerns my grandma would have had. And though this was the motivation I needed to take those first steps of faith, there were days that left me paralyzed just thinking back to my high school days.

I was a sophomore in high school when ED came into my life. We would sit together in the lunchroom. After lunch, all the kids would go into the library and hang out until the bell rang. But

ED would tell me no one really liked me; they were just being civil. He bragged that he was my only true friend. Everyone else would either be a danger to our secret or would just complicate priorities. So, we hung out together in the bathroom after lunch every day for years.

Some days, the mirrors would hang out with us. They were just as vocal. I was a prisoner on one hand but felt relieved on the other to not have to socialize. What would I bring to the table of conversation anyway? What did I have to offer anyone? Together, ED and I would plan our meals together, our exercise routines, and our exit strategies. We had work to do and socializing just interrupted important matters.

Thinking about those hours lost in the bathroom, I made the decision not to waste any more. I told Grandma I would look and see what groups the church had for kids my age. I was college-aged but not in college so I wasn't certain where I would fit. I called the church during the week and asked what classes they had on Sunday mornings for my age. The pastor directed me to a college and career class. And for a moment I was looking forward to making friends—real friends.

"Grandma, are you ready to go to church?" I said, having been ready for the last hour.

I woke up early that morning uncertain what I should wear. I used to plan out my outfits days, sometimes weeks in advance. But I learned that sometimes that would send me into panic attacks when things wouldn't fit like they used to. My eating habits would affect my body's composition. And some days I would be so bloated when

I woke up that things didn't fit right. This became an ongoing setup that left me emotionally unstable. I wouldn't learn for decades that I had a milk allergy that also contributed to my bloating and overnight disfigurement.

"Did you eat breakfast? I don't want you to be hungry an hour from now. It'll be at least three hours before lunch." Grandma responded.

I didn't mind being asked that question. In fact, I felt cared for and nurtured. I was healing and part of that process was letting people help me and stand in the gap for me.

"I'll just grab a banana. Thanks, Grandma," I said, trying to convey all my gratitude in a simple reply. And off we went to church.

Walking into my class, I had mixed emotions. Part of me was excited to be a blank slate again. No one knew me. No one knew my past, my struggles, my rebellion. But the other part of me was scared to be vulnerable for fear of being exposed. I knew that if I was going to settle down and plant roots, I would have to one day let people in to see my past, my struggles, and my rebellion.

"Hi, my name is Alora. I just moved here from North Dakota," I said by way of introduction.

"Welcome Alora. We're so glad you have decided to join us," the leader responded in a warm dad tone.

There were about 15 young people staring at me as I introduced myself. It's funny how our protective shields actually work against us. The timidness of my entry gave people the impression of me as one who was shy, scared, and possibly wounded. My shield became my give-away, but I still clung to it. In fact, my shield at times became my parachute. When I would feel like jumping out, I knew I would be protected. But there were a few people in that group who I instantly labeled in my mind as safe. Those were the ones I wanted to befriend.

The Beginning Of True Friendship

Was it her energy? Her compassion? Her love for Jesus? These were the questions I asked myself after being introduced to Gwen. She was confident and stable. I instantly gravitated toward her. She was silly and comfortable in her own skin. But when she sang and played her guitar, her childlike qualities turned into an angelic admiration and respect for God. Where did that unadulterated worship come from? How did one unite themselves so seamlessly into the presence of God and yet be moved by the same presence? All I knew was I wanted what she had, not in a covetous way but in a longing to be filled.

I found out that Gwen was a high school English teacher. She was just 20 years old and yet she was considered one of the best teachers in her school. However, she had her difficulties establishing the line between being friendly and demanding respect and authority. Many of the kids confided in her and she would take on the burdens of her students. At times she would be weighed down by them, but she learned to give the kids and their problems to Jesus. I think that was one of the disciplines she developed in her relationship with God. She would become the hands and feet of Christ, reaching a needy group of people: teenagers.

The college and career class was always doing something. Besides Sunday School and mid-week Bible study, we would go on trips. Our leader had a great way of recognizing our need for friendship and bonding as well as the greater need of sharing the gospel with them. We had game nights, all-nighters at the church, bonfires, and trips to the beach. But we also had service projects to raise money for missions. We had car washes, spaghetti dinners, and yard clean ups. This was foundational in building a new life with Christ. This was all for a purpose greater than I that God had promised me.

The following year the TV show *Friends* debuted. It was a sitcom focused on the interactions between six friends. We had an equal look into the life, problems, and relationships within the group. It was a show that we could relate to. By the time the show aired, I was part of a core group of about eight within the college and career group. We got together every week to watch *Friends*, eat food, and laugh our butts off.

But we soon learned that though we had some commonalities with *Friends*, we were on a different track. We were headed towards God, while *Friends* were headed for sex and sinful relationships. Lines eventually became blurred within our Christian circle and the things we used to live for were starting to resemble *Friends* and the world.

Chapter 11

The Nanny

A few days after I arrived at Grandma's house, I saw a help wanted ad for nannies in the local newspaper. I immediately called them and set up an interview a few days later. I felt like this was a door the Lord was opening, and I was going to walk through it. I didn't have a ready resume, so I asked Grandpa to help me build one. I was only 18 but I had been working since I was 13. I had already had four jobs that I would include, along with my years of babysitting during high school. As I worked with Grandpa to highlight my strengths, I drifted off into a memory.

During my high school years of babysitting, I was struggling with bulimia. Every house I would enter, I scanned their fridge and cupboards looking for food. As soon as I found what looked good, I would allow myself that treat after I did my job. This meant I would play with the kids, help them with their homework, get them ready for bed, and once in bed I would retreat to the kitchen for my reward. But this never ended with just one or two. Sometimes I would put a dent in whatever I chose. One house had frozen cookie dough balls, another had boxes of oatmeal crème pies, and still another ice cream. Looking back, I don't know why this was my routine. I just know that was my game plan for each gig.

"Alora, did you hear me?" Grandpa said in an annoyed tone.

"Oh, I'm sorry, Grandpa. I was just thinking about my strengths but couldn't come up with any that would be impressive on a resume," I said, trying to remain positive. I was determined not to let any negativity exude from me. I did not want to be sent home again.

"Well, I'm sure you have something you could put down. Since you're applying for a job to watch children, what are some experiences you had with that?" he asked, as if that's all the question entailed. For me, strengths were attached to success. And from where I was standing, I wasn't a success.

"Well, I guess I'm a caring person. I try to make sure everyone is having fun and is safe. Could that be something I could use, Grandpa?" I replied.

"It most definitely is," he encouraged.

We finished writing out my resume and filling out the application. Next, I needed to mail it in and wait. Waiting was the hard part. Should I continue looking? Do I continue applying and going on job interviews? What if I get offered something else but I haven't heard back about the nanny job? Grandpa said I could stay with them for as long as I needed. So he told me to wait a week and then start looking again.

Grandpa and I had a relationship but I wasn't as close to him as Grandma. He was seven years older than Grandma and his health wasn't that good. When I was younger, he took me out to the golf range once to teach me how to golf. I'm sure Grandma wanted him and I to bond over something. He loved golf. He would watch it on TV for hours. Jack Nicklaus was his favorite. He spent many hours on the golf course and even served as chairman of the Mt. Shadows Golf Committee. His most noted success in that arena was winning a trophy for making a hole in one.

My grandfather was an esteemed individual. He was vice president of a title company while serving as president of the Baptist Men's Club at their local church. But when it came to the kids, he kept his distance both physically and emotionally. So when it came to having any kind of male influence in my life, there wasn't much.

"Grandma! Grandma! I got a call from the nanny company. They scheduled an interview for me with a family who has three kids," I said, barely able to contain myself.

"Oh, Alora, that's wonderful. I know you're going to do so great. When's the interview?" Grandma replied in her usual positive way.

"It's this Saturday, just three days away. Oh my gosh, I'm so nervous," I anxiously responded, unable to keep my thoughts from running ahead of me.

"Ok, I can take you to it. I'll just stay in the car if that's ok with you," Grandma concluded.

"That should be fine. The lady told me this job would entail me living with them. They have a downstairs room with its own entrance. I guess it's like an in-law suite, but without a kitchen," I continued, getting even more excited as I talked about it.

"It's not too far away from you and Grandpa, so I'll still get to see you a lot. Oh and I would use their family van to haul the kids around. Oh my gosh, Grandma, this could be the best thing for me," I continued, daydreaming about the opportunities this job would provide.

"Well, anything you do, I know you'll be great at it. You just have to believe in yourself, Sweetheart," Grandma said as she left to finish up the laundry.

Probation With ED

By this time, I had cleaned up my act on the outside. I was going to church, making friends, being respectful to my grandparents, and almost had a job. But I was still battling an eating disorder. At this point, I wanted my relationship with ED to be over, but he wasn't ready to let me go. When I left Grandma's house a year earlier, I had been fearful to even gain a pound. I was skin and bones and still thought I was fat. And now, I was 50 pounds heavier. How did that happen? Well, the thing you need to know about eating disorders is that it's not about food but control. So whether I wasn't eating or I was binging, the control is what mattered. And even being out of control was still control focused.

Being bulimic was easier to blend in at social gatherings. There wasn't a need to keep tabs on me. But as an anorexic, people stared at me all the time. It was almost as if they needed to make sure

I would eat. And if I wasn't, they were quick to offer me food. When I was staying with Grandma and Grandpa, I would eat all the time. To them, this ensured I was healed. All they had known of my disorder before was not eating. So it was easy to fool them into believing I had recovered. But that unfortunately was far from the truth.

Four years into my eating disorder, it was no longer about having a secret. It wasn't about disappearing. It wasn't even about the weight. But it was about filling voids. At the time I had no idea what that even meant. All I knew is I found food to be a comfort. Whenever I was sad or depressed, I ate. Whenever I was happy, celebrations always included food.

The Interview

The day came for my interview. Grandma pulled up to the house and wished me good luck. She would be waiting for me when I was done. I took a deep breath and began the long walk up the steep driveway and up the L-shape flight of stairs. Breathing in one more time as I rounded the deck, I said a quick prayer.

"God. If You want me to work here, please help me with this interview." After saying amen, I felt more relaxed and rang the doorbell.

The dad opened the door and welcomed me in. Immediately, I could hear little kids giggling upstairs as they played with their toys. The kids soon found their way down to greet me as well. I'm sure it was a planned move to see how well we would connect from the beginning.

"Come in, Alora. I'm Brian and this is my wife, Kim," the dad said with a big smile.

"And these are our little ones. This one is Alex. He just turned five," Kim said with an even bigger smile. She was beautiful. She looked so young. I would later find out she was in her forties. "And this is Eric. He is our three-year-old. And this precious little girl is Angelina. She will turn one in a month."

"Hi guys. It's so nice to meet you. What do you have in your hand?" I said, looking at Alex.

"It's an airplane I made out of Legos," he said, as he began to fly it around the room in his hand.

"He loves Legos. He can spend hours in his room working on a project," Brian interjected, sounding like a proud dad.

"Well, boys can you take your sister upstairs and play in your room. We're going to talk with Alora for a little while. Then I'll come get you to say goodbye," Kim commanded, sounding firm yet loving.

And just like that they went upstairs. These kids were well behaved. That made me want the job even more. I was invited into their living room to begin the interview. I began by telling them how beautiful their house was. They told me they were in real estate and this was a new development. The neighborhood was pristine. Big, unique houses lined the streets. Not one of them were the same. As I marveled at the view from their living room window, I wished for this to be my house.

"So tell me, who would you say Alora is?" Brian kicked us off.

What an easy question for most people. But for me who had struggled the last four years with an identity crisis, I was almost paralyzed. Wait a minute, I thought to myself. This wasn't a question I rehearsed. You're supposed to ask me about my work experiences or maybe what I consider some of my strengths to be. Maybe a simple question of what I like and don't like. But to tell you who I am. I have no idea.

What I'm sure seemed like an eternity, was probably only a few seconds. Coming out of my head, I responded. "Well, I'm a work in progress. I was in a car accident last month that really shifted my priorities. I realized how important faith and family are. So I'm making the most out of every day," I responded, knowing God gave me the words for that answer.

"Wow, that's beautiful," Kim replied.

"So where are you currently staying?" she continued.

"I'm staying with my grandparents a few miles away. In fact, my grandma is waiting for me in the car," I replied.

"She's outside? Please, ask her to come in. I'd love to meet her," they both said, grinning from cheek to cheek.

I was happy to bring in the one person I loved with all my heart, the one woman who had been my champion through thick and thin. "Of course. I'll be right back," I said, as I got up and started to head for the door.

"Grandma! They want to meet you. Come on," I shrieked, excited to introduce the family to my family.

"They do? Well, okay let me get my purse," Grandma replied, sounding as anxious as I was.

"The kids are great, and the parents are so nice. You're going to love them," I said as we approached the door. With a little knock, we walked in.

There are moments in a person's life where the people you choose to have by your side will either help you or harm you. Many times, I had surrounded myself with people who were not good for me. And just the mere association with them hurt me in many ways. But that day, I knew Grandma would help me. She was the kindest woman I knew. Just her presence alone would calm my nerves.

I ended up getting the job and knew Grandma had a lot to do with it. Her warmth, her countenance, and her genuine heart all radiated off her. But one thing that sealed the deal was an answer to a question about discipline. Kim told me later that my answer was what won her over. She had asked me if I would ever spank her kids. I told her if that is what she would have me do, then I would do it. I told her that I would follow their plan for discipline. That way the correction was consistent no matter who was watching them. The punishment would always fit the crime, not the person. That way the kids would learn to respect me as much as their parents. But all the years I was their nanny, I never had to spank them. They were the best kids. I was so blessed to be their nanny.

Chapter 12

Spiritual And Physical Sickness

I found that I was making a home for myself in California. I had a lot of friends, a great family I worked for, and an extended family that I had reconnected with. I had never lived near my cousins, aunts, uncles, and grandparents growing up, especially after we left the state. It was weird to be surrounded with family when I couldn't tell you much about them.

My dad found Jesus when I was ten years old and immediately felt God was calling him into pastoral ministry. A year later he moved our family across the country to pastor a small church in Chandler, Illinois, about 20 minutes north of Briarfield. The heavy equipment and engine manufacturer, Caterpillar, was the largest employer in Briarfield. You couldn't drive anywhere without seeing CAT on something.

I wasn't excited to move, especially being pulled out of the middle of sixth grade to do so. I left the only area I had known with my friends, as well as being in the same state as Grandma. I changed that year. I started to become withdrawn, shy, and fearful of just showing up to school. I struggled making friends because I didn't talk. If they had given out awards at the end of year, I would have received the voted most likely not to be remembered trophy.

My dad came down with cancer a year after we moved to Illinois, even though he was in the prime of his life. He was 45 years old and in good health, but was diagnosed with stage 4 T-cell non-Hodgkin lymphoma. The doctor opened him up, saw the invasion of cancer, and gave him 45 days to live. That day, my father, who was already emotionally distant, moved even more inward, rarely coming out of hiding.

I don't have any memories of my father being sick. I have seen the pictures of how the cancer or the chemo, or both, destroyed my father. Once a strong and commanding police officer, I saw him broken down to a weak and depressed victim. I don't even have a 30-second clip revealing my father's pain. Loss of hair, dark circles under his eyes, weight loss, vomiting continually, constant cold sores in his mouth, weakness, and non-stop nausea not to mention the intense pain he felt on a daily basis—all were removed from my memory. I can't imagine how they could hide that from a 12-year-old. So as time went on, so did my memories.

In the agony of his pain, my father pleaded with the Lord to heal him. He begged for his life to be spared long enough to watch his children grow up, get married, and have children of their own.

Then, the Lord could take him. That prayer eventually was answered according to my father's pleas but not before a move took place.

"James, I believe if you had more faith you would be healed by now," the district superintendent of my father's denomination said. Those words were as powerful as a gunshot wound to the heart and they hit my father's ears in disbelief.

This careless and hateful statement changed the trajectory of my entire life. Shortly after this brief interaction, my father put in a transfer request to go to another district. And just like that, I found myself moving again. Luckily, I got to finish out middle school before moving. But during that summer we moved to Ashford, North Dakota. I had no choice. This would be my fifth move in my short life, and one that would continue shaping me into the person I am today.

To this day, to not remember a day of my father's lowest point of his life causes me some consternation. But I find comfort in knowing that Jesus was there by his side every day of his torment. And even if I can't remember anything, I'm sure there were days I sat and just held his hand. That I choose to forge as a memory.

Grandma's Strength

Grandma was throwing another family gathering at her house the weekend after I started my new job. I had just moved out and even though it had only been a week, I was glad to be staying with Grandma for the weekend. I loved it when she would gather the family, assign Grandpa to the grill, and make her famous desserts. Her Watergate Coverup was by far my favorite. I don't know if it was the rich chocolate or the smooth texture of the pudding that made it my favorite. Maybe it was the airy whipped topping or the crunchy graham cracker crust. As a child, I had no clue about the real Watergate coverup so as I got older and learned about the events that took place in our government, I had to chuckle.

Grandma was the glue who held the family together. She was the hub, the core. She found any excuse to throw a dinner party or a celebration in her backyard. She loved entertaining, and she loved family. She would invite her three brothers and their families along with their families over. Her dear friend, June, who she had been friends with for more than 40 years, was someone who never needed an invitation. She was always welcome. We all called her Aunty June. Grandma loved tending to her flower beds and watching them bloom in the spring. Her flowers became a staple decoration. She was passionate about gardening and her hard work paid off every year.

But I wonder what secrets those flower beds kept for Grandma; how many rose bushes were watered by her tears? As she pruned the shrubbery, would she reflect on the times when God had pruned her? When she would throw out flowers that had expired, would she recall the times she felt just as expired? Grandma was a strong woman, but I know there were days her heart bled before God Almighty, especially when her only biological son was suffering with cancer—multiple times.

Staying with Grandma never lacked a tour through her hope chests. Every year visiting them as children, we would make a bee line for the hope chests and look through them. She had two big ones that were filled with treasures: old fashioned pictures, baby books, handmade outfits we all wore as toddlers, newspaper clippings of stories from decades past, and old letters from Dad when he was in the Vietnam War. She even had some Norwegian items from her heritage: a doll, postcards, nicknacks, and Norwegian currency.

After her death, I was willed one of these treasured chests. I can only imagine the secrets this treasure chest held. With every contribution Grandma would make to this chest, there would be a little girl fascinated by it. She would never learn of the tears I shed reading through the letters between her and Dad. The chest started collecting secrets for me as well.

Repeated Past

It's scary how far one can drift while imitating presence. Some would call it hypocrisy. I had found a close knit group of friends to whom I began to let in. We attended church together, went on weekend getaways, and one day found ourselves going to the bar together. Physical relationships started to form within the group and the goal posts of pleasing God started to move an inch here and an inch there.

The emotional voids I had filled with alcohol, bulimia, and boys in the past started to reappear. And before you knew it, I was seeped in bulimia again, making out with church guys, and drinking on the weekends. The only difference now were the people I hung out with were Christians. The previous shame from rebellion was now replaced with current shame from hypocrisy. My secret life was resurrected and who would be waiting? ED.

Oh, the hamster wheels we find ourselves on, running so fast and so hard to get nowhere. I was jeopardizing my future and the people I was closest to were starting to get concerned. You can only hide for so long before the ones you let in start sniffing around. By then I had been struggling with bulimia for eight long years and my façade was starting to deteriorate. I was what some would call a carnal Christian.

That meant that I loved Jesus, but I loved myself more. I found that every decision I made was based on my desires, ambitions, wants, and control. Prayer was a flare to ignite after an accident happened—a call for help. I knew God had saved me once. Could He, or better yet, would He want to rescue me again?

"Alora, we have to talk," Mom said over the phone one spring afternoon. She and dad were still living in North Dakota.

"Ok, you sound worried. Is everything okay?" I responded, trying not to think the worse.

"It's about your dad. He has cancer again," she tried saying but it only came out as a whisper.

"What kind?" I replied, trying not to overreact.

"Prostate," Mom said, her voice cracking knowing this type of cancer can be lethal.

"What is the plan? What do the doctors want to do?" I said, sniffling now and allowing myself to react.

"Dad is scheduled for surgery in Minnesota

in a few weeks. They think the cancer is contained and will be able to get it all when they remove his prostate," Mom continued.

"Well, I've been doing a lot of thinking. I've been done with my nanny job here for the last six months and I've just been feeling like I need a change of scenery. With Dad's prognosis, could I move in with you guys for a year? I could help with taking care of Dad," I pleaded, knowing I needed a change one way or the other.

"That would actually be wonderful, Alora. I'll be in touch with how Dad's surgery goes," Mom said as she hung up the phone.

And with the click of the phone, my life was once again changed forever. I broke down in tears. The memories of my father's last bout with cancer had to have come rushing back into my body like a tidal wave, just missing my mind. I still couldn't remember the early days of his suffering, but my body did, and it went right to work building a construct of safety and protection around myself.

A few weeks later, my parents drove 12 hours to the Veterans Hospital in St. Paul. They spent the night in a hotel to rest up for the early morning surgery. The next morning, while sitting in the waiting room to be prepped for surgery, my parents were called in to speak to the oncologist.

"Mr. Walker, I'm sorry to tell you that we have to postpone the prostate surgery," the doctor began to explain.

"What? We just drove 12 hours to get here. Why?" My dad snapped back, adrenaline pumping through him from the already present anxiety for the surgery.

"After examining your cat scan pictures, we discovered a large tumor on your right kidney," the doctor calmly responded, as he hung up the x-rays for them to see.

He continued pointing to the x-ray, "Here you have an earlier cat scan that shows a very small spot on your kidney. In all probability, that spot was mislabeled as a cyst and ignored. But look at the recent scan. Do you see how much it has grown in such a short time? I still have to discuss my findings with the other oncologist, but it appears we will have to remove your right kidney instead of your prostate."

A short time later, it was determined my dad would have to have his kidney removed, and a treatment plan for removing his prostate would follow. My mother called me that day giving me the bad news. There was no doubt in my mind that I needed to be with my family. I made arrangements to move out that summer

Chapter 13

Jesus Revealed

"I will be back in one year! Don't forget about me," I told my friends as I was moving back home to North Dakota. I meant it this time. Not like a I hope to or if everything works out kind of way. No, I was dead serious. No longer were my friends disposable. I had planted roots. I had been vulnerable with them. I invested six years of my life into these friendships. I was coming back if it was the last thing I did.

My plan was to move in with my parents in Moby, North Dakota for a year and I would get a job and start saving my money. Living in California was pretty expensive since I had ended my job as a nanny and moved out. And by then, I figured Dad would be back to health. I left that day determined to make this happen.

The trip to my parents would take 25 hours. I would complete it by car in three days. I had my hotels already reserved and knew exactly where the rest areas were on my map. This was the first trip I would be taking on my own. There was no one following me making sure I stayed on the road, or riding cross-country on the train like I had a few times before. No, this time was just me and the road. I was 23 years old and taking another detour. I had hit the pause button on life in California. Would my friends do the same or would their lives go on without me? I had my concerns, but I also had the fight in me to do my part.

Living the "Christian" life was becoming more difficult to sustain. I realized I knew nothing more of God than when I had arrived. I had insulated myself in a Christian bubble that made it easy to blend in when I was sinning. It almost made it okay since all the other Christian young adults were doing it! But Gwen was different. When others were singing praise songs, she was worshiping the one whom we sang to. When we gathered for Bible study, she came to learn more about God while we wanted to chill with our friends. And when a few of us turned 21 and wanted to start going to bars to get wasted, she let us know her true feelings on the issue.

Not everyone in the group was as carnal as I was. Maybe I was the one who was the bad influence and turned others toward sin. I had a desire to be loved and accepted, and interested boys fulfilled that desire. Drinking, dancing, making out, and seeking my own things were the portrait of who I was the day I left. The only difference between the 17-year old girl who was totally wasted in her sister's bathtub, clothes on, was that now I had a halo above my head. It's amazing how one can live under the radar for so long that you fool everyone into believing you're someone that you're not. But there was one person I couldn't fool. One who knew everything that I was doing and yet still loved me, accepted me, and noticed me, and that was Jesus!

A few hours into my trip, out of the blue, Jesus spoke. I didn't hear Him with my ears but with my heart—and it was loud. Instantly I felt the Lord's presence fill my car. He was so tangible and evident. And one by one, God removed the blinders from my eyes, the scales, the spiritual cataracts that had blurred my vision of who God truly was through the person of Jesus Christ.

Within moments of this awakening, I was flooded with truth—that Jesus wanted to be my friend, my Savior, my Redeemer and not just for that day but for the rest of my life. Tears followed as I confessed every sin I could think of that I had justified or rationalized. He invited me in to follow Him, and I said yes.

I had heard of Jesus my entire life, but I had never before encountered Him. I was the one sheep that had wandered from the flock. I was the lost coin that was being searched for. I was the prodigal child who was living life in a pig's pen. I was Hagar in the desert who went into hiding. I was Lot in Sodom and Gomorrah who was trapped. I was the blind man who had never seen the light.

Before I even knew I was lost, I was found. I never realized I needed rescued. I didn't know I couldn't see. But when Jesus rode shotgun with his search light radiantly shining into my soul, He revealed my need to see, to be released, and be saved. And just by saying yes to Him, I came alive. Joy came pouring in. Purpose surfaced.

Love overflowed. God had met me again in my car but this time it wasn't to save my life but to save my soul.

I spent the next three days holding His hand and talking for hours to my new friend. I went from believing in God to knowing God because He continued to talk as well. He filled my soul with truth about Himself. He told me how much He loved me. And He set my feet on a new path. Hope was restored and I couldn't wait to share this with my family.

I was realizing that every time I came back home or departed, I would be going or coming as a different person. This time would be no different. However, this time I would be coming home the person God made me to be. I would not be trying on a new identity to see if it fit better than the last one. But rather I would be coming home a whole new person—from the inside out. I had been looking my whole life for a way out but now, as a new creation in Christ, I was brought in and there was no other place I wanted to be.

The day God rescued me from my sinking car, I told Him I was going back to church, and getting back in line. The day I was resurrected, I buried my list of do's and don'ts. I traded in my halo for the cross. I would from that point on depend on Him through His Spirit to lead me. I would no longer follow my own reasoning. I was truly born again, and no one was going to change my decision to follow Jesus.

What Is God Up To?

I arrived at my parents on the third day and met up with my family at a local restaurant for dinner. My sister, Diane, also joined us. She had recently moved to Moby, the town where Mom and Dad lived. Our relationship could be described as a roller coaster or an erratic EKG—up and down and tumultuous at times. By this time, we were at a better place. We spent the evening reconnecting and talking about Dad and his recovery. He had already had both surgeries—six weeks apart from each other—and had healed up nicely from both. He was strong again. He was free again. And this was going to be our time.

The following week, after unpacking and getting settled into my new living quarters, I started to apply for jobs. There was a new company in town called CompuTech that was paying top dollar to its technicians. My brother-in-law was working there and said he'd put in a good word for me. CompuTech was a call center that provided tech support for Gateway computers and customer service for a few major credit card companies. I knew nothing about computers but since they offered on-the-job training, I decided to apply.

"I can't believe I got the job," I said in disbelief to my family a few weeks later.

"Congratulations, Alora! That's wonderful news," my mom replied.

Reflecting on the job interview, I knew God was up to something because there was no way I should've gotten hired. When asked if I knew what Windows was, I pointed to the glass pane. When asked if I knew what a PC was, I said I did not, but I followed it up with 'But I am a quick learner.' I left that interview thinking two things. Either God translated my words to make my it sound like 'personal computer' or the cleavage I inadvertently wore worked to my advantage. There is no way I would have hired me—but they did. And so, I was determined to learn all I could.

I finished my two weeks of training and moved into my cubicle. I had never worked in a cube before. I liked having a space all my own while being near to a community of help. I hung up pictures of my friends and family and put on my headset. Like the adrenaline prior to jumping off a diving board, I took a deep breath then pressed the button to start taking calls.

"I don't have any picture on my screen," said one customer, frantic because she was in the middle of writing a paper.

"My cup holder isn't coming out," another lady complained, which made me scratch my head.

"Hello, dear. I'm sorry to bother you, but I just can't seem to get my keyboard to work," a man said, as I pondered if he had it plugged in.

"You have to help me figure out the sound? Nothing is coming out of the speakers," a teenager complained, who was rushing me because he needed his jams.

All these calls came flooding in within my first few hours. And these weren't just calls I could say to push this button or call this number. No, I had to walk these people through getting into the meat of their desktops.

"Ok, so grab a flathead screwdriver and let me know when you're back. Then, unscrew the 10 screws holding your computer together and take the lid off. Then, dig through the yellow, green, and blue wires until you see the red wire. Follow that all the way to the motherboard and make sure it's connected firmly. Reset cables, remove the RAM, and wait 10 seconds then put it back in, plug this into here and that into there." It was crazy. Some of these people were in their seventies and eighties!

Then we would have to walk our customers through uninstalling and reinstalling new software. Upload programs, download patches, and if that didn't work, I would have to find parts and order them for the customers. Looking back now, I know God used a remote access and remote-control computer software to take over my mind and mouth.

We had a team of tech leads who would be waiting for us newbies to raise our white flag when we were in over our heads or out of options. When our flag was raised, they would come over and either give us the solution to instruct our customer with or point us in the direction to find the tools ourselves. I always liked the first option because by the time I would retreat, I had already searched the online tools. But these guys were so helpful and never made us feel stupid for even asking. I learned to value their expertise and respect their knowledge. One of those guys was named Caleb.

Chapter 14

An Unexpected Blessing

"Hey, I'm getting a tattoo after work. Would you like to come with me?" Caleb casually asked one day during work.

"Really, what are you getting?" I asked excitedly. Not that he specifically asked me out but that I had recently gotten a tattoo before I moved back home and hadn't gotten to see how they did it. Mine was right above my hip bone and so I had to lay down for the whole procedure.

"Well, it's this triangular shape with circles that I drew up one night. It's hard to explain," he said, realizing he himself had no idea what it was or what it meant. I later learned that he drew it one night when he was drunk.

"Cool. I should be able to go." And that was later deemed as our first date. However, at the time, I had told myself that boys were out of the question.

On the first day of my trip when Jesus chose to reveal Himself to me, I decided that my attention and priority were going to be on Him. Family would be next in line. I had spent the last six years of my life chasing after boys hoping for fulfillment, acceptance, love, and wholeness only to realize those years were wasted because I was looking in all the wrong places. The other reason I didn't want to get involved with anyone in North Dakota was because I wasn't planning on staying there longer than a year. My home was in California. I had a plan and even though Jesus was now a part of it, I was still set on moving after a year.

"Are you crying?" I laughingly asked Caleb as the needle imprinted on his skin.

"I might be tearing up but I'm not crying," he responded.

Taking a break, we got to talking and found that we clicked right away. He was funny, witty, and very sarcastic. I felt comfortable with him even though I didn't even know his last name. We bounced off each other like we were volleying. I wasn't nervous around him. In fact, I felt like I could be myself, even though I wasn't really sure who that was yet.

"Want to grab a bite to eat?" Caleb asked after he was done.

"Sure, I could eat," I responded.

We left for Applebee's not thinking much of it. A girl has to eat, right? On the way there I felt safe. Maybe it was because I knew this guy didn't have a chance with me. I wasn't interested in turning this into something. I enjoyed having guy friends and Caleb would be added to my list. I had gone out to eat dozens of times with my guy friends without a problem, so I didn't feel weird about it.

As we sat down and continued our conversation, things started getting deep. He talked about his family and the drama that was associated with them. I talked about my father's illness and the reason I moved out here. I talked about my on-again off-again relationship with my sister, Diane, and he talked about his time in the military and how he had just gotten out that spring. We definitely clicked and I really enjoyed talking with him. It was nice to have a friend since I was beginning to get homesick for my friends back home.

Jesus First

AOL Instant Messaging was a big thing in the '90s, and that became our platform for communicating. We would be on there for hours just talking about life—past, present, and future. One day Caleb asked the forbidden question!

"So, if you were looking for a boyfriend, what qualities would he have to possess in order for you to date him?" He asked sheepishly.

"Well, number one, he has to be a Christian," I stated in a matter-of-fact manner. I'm sure I continued on with my list, but Caleb's ears didn't follow.

Hmm, a Christian. Caleb knew he was disqualified in just the first round.

"A Christian, huh?" he replied.

"Yep. I take my faith very seriously," I responded just as matter of fact.

"Well, could I go to church with you this Sunday?" Caleb said, stunned by his own question.

"Are you wanting to go for me or for you?" I asked, with a little flirtatiousness in my voice.

"A little of both," he said, and that was that.

He showed up that Sunday, not realizing that decision would change the direction of his life forever.

He later would tell me that he showed up that morning so early that the only people there were the janitor and the preacher. He had served eight years in the Air Force and punctuality was engraved in him from day one. If something starts at 9 a.m. and he arrived at 9 a.m., he was late. If he arrived at 8:45 a.m., he was considered on time. And if he arrived at 8:30 a.m., only then was he early. Caleb loved to be early for things, so he waited for me and my family to arrive.

While he waited and people started to file in, he began to get sweaty and nervous. He believed all his sins were written on his forehead for everyone to read. He had recently come from a pretty dark place in his life and coming into the light exposed that to him. The Lord was already at work in him and he was starting to feel uncomfortable.

"Caleb, hi!" I said, waving at him from across the foyer.

"Good morning," Caleb excitedly replied, walking toward my family and me.

We filed into the sanctuary to take our seat. Church was part of my DNA but it was the opposite for Caleb. Fellowship, prayer, worship, communion, Bible, sermon, altar call, confession, tithes, testimonies, and amens were all foreign to him. When do you sit, when do you stand? When do you talk, what do you say? When do you go up the aisle, do you have to? All these rituals to an unbeliever have to be confusing and intimidating, almost like being in a foreign country trying to speak English when they all speak their native language. How does one bridge the gap?

"So, did you like it?" I asked Caleb, as we walked out into in the parking lot.

"Yeah, I did. Thanks for letting me come," he replied, uncertain he believed his own words.

"Do you want to come back next Sunday?" I asked. To me, faith was my foundation. I loved Jesus and wanted everyone else to as well. And Jesus went to church. So if I wanted Caleb to know about Jesus, I wanted him to be in the same room as Him. (This was my elementary understanding of God at the time).

"Sure," he said, as he got in his car and drove off.

Getting Serious

We continued spending a lot of time with each other at work and after work. I was beginning to become emotionally invested with Caleb. He was such a great friend, but I was beginning to think he was becoming more than that to me. Caleb never thought of me as just a friend. He was always hoping something would become of us, so he never settled for friendship in his mind.

By this point, my faith was becoming even more solid, so to date someone who wasn't a believer did not make sense to me. Therefore, I started praying for his salvation. Looking back now it was 50% selfish and 50% selfless. Of course, I wanted him to have this awesome relationship with Jesus like I had and have the assurance of eternal life in heaven. But I also wanted to protect myself from an unequally yoked relationship. I spent a lot of time in prayer that fall.

At the same time, I was still battling my addiction with bulimia. I was beginning to think that no matter how strong my faith was, ED was stronger. Caleb and I had gotten pretty close, so I shared with him one night after we decided to start dating each other that I had bulimia and that I was trying to beat it.

"I can't be with anyone who would intentionally hurt themselves." Caleb said, sounding half disgusted and half fearful.

"I know I can beat it. I promise I won't throw up anymore. You mean so much to me. I'd hate for this to come in between us," I replied, not sure if I could deliver on my promise but knowing I would try my hardest.

Caleb continued to attend church with me for about a month. And every Sunday, the pastor would give an altar call for anyone wishing to be prayed over for healing, confession, or salvation. And every Sunday, I was trying to will Caleb to walk down the aisle in my head. But every Sunday he remained in his seat. I didn't know what was happening in his heart. I just saw him remain seated.

By this time, I had fallen in love with Caleb and feared the risk I was taking was more than I could handle. I had many conversations with God about my decision to date Caleb. I was scared and confused. But I felt an overwhelming peace to remain in this relationship. I felt God was telling me it would be ok and to just trust Him.

The Proposal

"Lord, I know Caleb is going to propose tonight. I'm so scared. He hasn't said 'yes' to you yet.

I don't know what I should do. If I say 'yes' to his proposal, am I disobeying you? But if I tell him 'no,' I feel like I'm going against these emotions I believe You're in. And it's not like I could say 'yes, contingent upon his salvation.' Please tell me what to do." As soon as I stopped talking, I felt a peace within telling me to say 'yes' and that it would be okay. God would work all things out.

That night we stayed in to watch a movie, *City of Angels*. We cuddled on the couch and laughed and cried. Then, just as the movie came to an end, Meg Ryan's character and Nicholas Cage's character finally fall in love. We assumed they would ride off into the sunset together, completely happy and fulfilled. But out of nowhere, Meg Ryan's character gets hit by a Mac truck! "Are you kidding me?"

But before those four words came out of my mouth, Caleb looked at me and said, "I don't want another second to go by without asking you to spend the rest of your life with me. Alora, will you marry me?" Caleb proposed, as he stared in my eyes waiting for my response.

Without missing a beat, I said yes! I had received assurance from God that all would work out. And that was all I needed to trust Him. I loved Caleb and I wanted to be with him. We held each other tight and started to plan our lives together.

He was living with his roommate in a two-bedroom apartment at the time. I, of course, was living 40 minutes away with my parents. We talked about getting our own apartment after we got married or moving away. I had told him that my desire was to eventually move back to

California. But by that point, he meant more to me than my plans. So I packed that thought away and focused on our wedding.

Chapter 15

Our Special Day

Weddings are the most beautiful events to watch—the flowers, the music, the dress, the vows, the kiss! But the build up to that beautiful, magical day can be the most stressful and ugly series of events imaginable—the decisions, the guest list, the bills, and the family, and in my case, the fear of marrying an unbeliever.

Caleb and I started a pre-marriage counseling course at our church with our pastor after we were engaged. This was a requirement our pastor had for any couple he would marry. If he didn't feel they were ready to get married or if things came up that went against his beliefs, he would have the right to bow out of officiating.

At the start of our session, Caleb wasn't a believer. And this was one of the first questions that came up. Caleb wasn't the type of person who would do something just to get by. He had respect for faith and would never just say he was something he wasn't. But he was definitely thinking hard about Christianity. Our pastor gave him a video on the life of Jesus and encouraged him to watch it that week. Then we would meet up the following week.

I had been praying for Caleb to surrender to Jesus. I knew life apart from Christ and I knew life in Christ. It was day and night—literal light versus darkness. I wanted him to experience the light. I wanted that so badly for Caleb and for us, but I knew it was a decision only Caleb could make.

I was never the little girl who had a scrapbook full of wedding designs and color swatches. I hadn't dreamt of what my wedding dress would look like. I didn't have my color scheme, or my flower arrangements predetermined. I had no dream honeymoon reserved for that special day. I didn't have my vows written and stored in a keepsake box.

I was a realist. It wouldn't have surprised me if I never got married. I spent my entire life feeling unworthy and unwanted so why would I think the fairytale weddings would've ever come true for me? My bar was set really low. Having my best friend propose was a fairytale come true, so it didn't matter what we wore or what we ate. I didn't care about the location or the reception. All that mattered was that Caleb showed up and said yes!

All I knew about relationships, specifically marriages, was that they were hard work that most often didn't work out. My grandmother's first marriage to my father's dad ended in divorce after a decade of violence. My mother and father's rocky relationship full of trust issues and emotional affairs almost did them in. My sister Diane's abusive relationship later ended in infidelity and divorce. My other sister's abusive and cheating husband wouldn't let her leave, so she left in the middle of the night with their daughter and divorced years later. And that was just on my side.

Caleb's parent's divorced when he was four years old. His dad went on to remarry three more times and divorce twice. His mom remarried an abusive alcoholic who beat Caleb. After their divorce, she remarried again. And his sister's boyfriend left her after he got her pregnant, leaving her to raise their daughter alone.

But even though this was the marital pedigree we both came from, we were confident we would break the generational divorce chain and start a new chain of a loving, devoted, and honest marriage. We made a commitment to each other that no matter how hard life got, we would never threaten divorce.

"I gave my life to Jesus today," Caleb said over Chinese one night.

"What? Are you serious? That's wonderful," I said, exhaling as if I just had a close call.

"Yeah, you know that Jesus video Pastor Jim gave me last week after our counseling? Well, I watched it and it all made sense. So I got down and knelt by my couch and asked Him in," Caleb said matter of fact.

"I'm so happy for you—for us!" I replied.

The decision to follow Jesus is one of the most important and personal decisions anyone can make in their life. It not only affects their current life but their eternal life. The moment you say yes to Jesus, you are crossing over from death to life. And that day I was relieved my soon-to-be husband was alive!

We were elated when we went to Pastor Jim a few days later for our next session. Caleb was glowing. He had so many questions but felt so free. Jim talked with us about baptism—what it was, what it did, and what it didn't do. We decided to get baptized together the following month. I had been sprinkled as an infant in the Catholic Church and dunked in the Nazarene Church after my father got saved, but neither time was my choice. But now I understood the meaning of baptism. Going under the water symbolized that I was dying to myself and rising out of the water represented me being raised to new life with Christ. I was definitely ready to proclaim my love for Jesus and my desire to follow Him anywhere.

As I pondered baptism, I couldn't help but remember my submersion under the waters six years earlier. Both would result in surrender. However, one was motivated by fear while the other was motivated by love. I was in a good place. However, there were some hiccups along the way during the wedding planning.

The Rumblings

I had heard all about wedding drama and wanted to steer clear of it. So, I decided to ask my sister, Diane, to be my maid of honor. She had always been jealous of my relationship with my other sister, Lauren, growing up. Even as adults, she hated seeing us so close. I knew if I asked Lauren to be my maid-of-honor, it would blow up in my face. So Lauren was a bridesmaid along with my friends, Gwen and LeAnn.

I hated that I felt like I had to avoid a potential upset by my abusive sister. This was supposed to be my special day with the love of my life but I still found myself living in the shadows of the boogey man. But the reality was that my sister was a ticking time bomb. I could feel the rumblings but sometimes there wasn't enough time to make the necessary adjustments before getting hit by shrapnel. And when I would get hit, the cycle would go something like this:

> "I'm so sorry, Alora. Can you forgive me? I love you so much. We're blood. And blood is thicker than water. It's the Christian thing to do," Diane would say after her emotional assaults on me.

> "Diane, I'm getting really tired of this. You can't just keep wounding me and apologize when you've cooled off expecting me to keep forgiving you and allowing you to come back into my life. This has got to stop," I would cry in complete exasperation.

> "I know. I don't know why I get so upset at you. You're my baby sister and I love you so much. I promise I won't ever hurt you again," Diane would promise.

> "This is literally the last time I'll forgive you," I would say, hoping I would never be hurt again.

I knew giving in was my specialty. Deep down I knew that my response was really an empty threat. How could I ever be strong enough to walk away? All I ever knew was abuse—emotional, physical, and mental. But I sure did hope she was serious, because if she was serious, then I would never again have to be weak and give in to the boogey man.

A month into the wedding planning, Diane threw a grenade, and I was left picking up the pieces. I never understood why I continuously believed my sister's apologies. Was it naivete? Was it hope that Diane had changed? Was it my own mental illness that kept me in bondage? Did I enjoy the pain in some sadistic way?

I was used to taking cover when I felt the rumblings. Nothing would disrupt her plans but at least I could see it coming. It was worse when it came out of the blue. It's like when you fall down. If you catch yourself with your hands, your hands get banged up but you save your face. It still hurts but not as bad as it would falling flat on your face. But this day, I had no time to catch myself.

Diane had just apologized for something that had happened earlier in the week. Most of her attacks have been filed away in my brain that I haven't been able to access my whole life—except for this one. I remember this attack like it was minutes ago. She apologized, I forgave her. Same cycle. She asked if I wanted to go into town to do some shopping. I thought this would be a good way to move on. We all make mistakes, right?

I said I would drive and we made our way out of the small town our parents lived in. We got on a 10-mile stretch of road that led us to the shopping mall. Out of the blue Diane looked at me with pure hate and disgust and said, "I hope Caleb beats you to death and that you go to hell.

Because when I get to Heaven, I don't want to see you there."

Instantly I felt trapped. There was nowhere to hide. Nowhere to run. She was literally three feet away from me. I made a u-turn right there on the narrow road and headed back to Mom and Dad's house. I couldn't get back home quick enough. I was in shock. I was scared. I was muted. I couldn't move. I could barely breathe. It felt like the wind had been knocked out of me. I blocked out the rest of what was said, if anything. I couldn't understand why she hated me so much. I told myself this was the last time she would ever hurt me again. I was so set on never seeing her again. I wanted to rid myself of her.

Victimization is hard to overcome. I so badly wanted to walk away, but I couldn't. In a weird way, I felt sorry for her. All my life I was told "that's just Diane" and she couldn't help being who she is. Was she a victim herself? Was she being held captive by her disease? Was her trauma as a child making her do and say these horrible things? Are words that bad? Did she really mean it? I decided to just demote her from being my maid of honor to just being a guest at my wedding. We had to find another bridesmaid last minute to fill out the wedding party. By the time the wedding came, all I cared about was marrying Caleb and starting our lives together far away in California.

I Do

Dad walked me down the aisle on March 14, 1999. As I walked toward the man with whom I would spend the rest of my life, my six-foot train followed in succession. My eyes locked on Caleb as I stepped one foot in front of the other. I couldn't believe my day had come. Would I fulfill all his dreams? Would I be enough for him? Could this refurbished vessel satisfy him for the long haul?

"Who gives this bride in marriage?" our pastor asked as the wedding began.

"Her mother and I do," Dad proudly responded. Lifting my veil, he kissed me on the cheek and handed me to my bridegroom. Then my father tagged our preacher out and began to officiate our wedding.

Gazing into each other's eyes, we couldn't stop smiling. This was our moment. Despite the obstacles that preceded this day, we would become one. Our life as Mr. and Mrs. Stone began that day, and our commitment to each other was that it would last for our entire lives. We vowed we would stick by each other through sickness and in health; through poverty and riches; and not that it was said, but in family drama that we knew would find its way in our marriage.

Moving Day

"I put a transfer into California," Caleb said one night after his shift.

"You did?" I excitedly responded.

"Yeah, it's not Santa Elia, but close in Sacramento. Are you okay with that?" he asked.

"I am. Thank you, Babe. I love you so much," I replied, exhaling again.

We planned to move to California that fall. That would be a little over a year since I had moved there. I thought about my original plan, the one that didn't include boys because I didn't want to get stuck in North Dakota. I realized then that planning my life according to my wants, abilities, and assumptions was no way to live for Jesus. If I was truly wanting to follow Jesus, I would have to write my plan in pencil, pray, and wait for Him to tell me when and where to go.

As I sat and reflected on the previous year, I was amazed at how the Lord had lined everything up for me to be in the right place at the right time to meet Caleb. He had worked through the job interview, through my rigid plans, and through Caleb's heart to bring us together. And through it, Caleb became a child of God!

We wanted to start a family right away. Caleb was 26 years old and though I was just 24, I felt like I had lived 50 years already and was ready to build my family. I found out I was pregnant two months after our wedding. I was elated. I had been bulimic free for nine months by that time and now that I was pregnant, ED was the furthest thing from my mind. I was set on taking care of myself better than I had ever done before because now I was growing a baby inside of me. It was not only my body, but a shared body. ED faded to the background and joy rose to the front. I had married the love of my life and was now carrying his child. There was nothing that could replace what I had.

Chapter 16

Brenna – Promise Of God

"It's a girl!" the doctor said as he rubbed the wand of the ultrasound machine across my belly.

As tears welled up in my eyes, I immediately felt a connection to the life inside of me. I had already picked out her name—Brenna Rose Stone. The little girl I was a nanny for had a friend named Brenna and I loved that name. Before I even met Caleb, I wanted to name my first girl Brenna. Caleb was so sweet and said I could name her anything I wanted if it was a girl but if it was a boy, he would get to name him. So right away we began calling our little pea Brenna, Bree for short.

By now we were living in a suburb of Sacramento, California. Caleb had transferred to the Hewlett-Packard call center and was working as a manager. I was also able to get a job there doing tech support. I was planning on working up until I had Brenna and then go back to work six weeks after she was born.

I was glad to be back in California. I had already made the trip to Santa Elia to visit my family and friends, a two-hour trip. Grandma threw a welcome home party for us and it was great seeing all my family again. I especially loved introducing Caleb to Grandma. She had been the most important person in my life for so long but now that spot would be shared. She was fine with that because she could see how happy I was. She too remembered what my life was like not that long before.

We were also closer to Caleb's side of the family. He was born and raised in the Pacific Northwest near Seattle, Washington. His family was scattered over the state but after the wedding, we made a point to visit them. Everyone was ecstatic for Brenna to make her entrance. We were married, had a child on the way, growing in our faith, and were now 25 hours away from my sister. I could relax and not have to walk on eggshells around her like I had for the previous year and a half.

As you enter new stages in your life, the friends you have often go with you but sometimes they don't. I had been the first one in our friend circle to get married. Everyone else had remained in California and was either dating or just single. And I was two hours away with a baby on the way. The only one who remained in my circle for the long haul was Gwen. She was so much like Caleb. In fact, some days I thought I married Gwen. We stayed in touch, she visited, and when my babies came into this world, she would become their godmother. She truly was an angel who God sent to me. She walked many paths with me and had to go searching for me when I went down some other paths. I was blessed to have her in my life.

Reflecting on the kind of mother I would

be to Brenna, I knew I would do everything in my power to protect her. I knew the kind of scary world we lived in. And I made a vow to myself that I would show her how much I loved her. I would say it and show it. There was nothing more important to me than fulfilling my commitments I had made to myself, my child, my husband, and my God. I had been recycled for a greater purpose and my big belly was part of it.

Caleb tells me that I must have amnesia concerning our first year of marriage because I thought it was great! I knew we had a few squabbles, but other than that, I remembered I was so happy. But apparently, we both threw out the 'D' word (divorce) a few times in that first year. I blame it on the hormones and baby brain. He later told me he knew we would last forever because if we could make it through our first year, we could make it through every year.

They say the big stressors in a relationship are a new job, a move, a baby, and a death. And at that point we had three out of four going on at the same time. I knew our marriage had survived by God and God alone. He surely had His hand on us. I wonder if the angel that sat watch over me in Wyoming was the same one keeping watch over our marriage? Would there be an expiration date on angel duty? I sure hoped not. I needed God's protection, strength, and forgiveness daily.

False Labor

"Get out!!" I screamed at Brenna. I was a week overdue and was miserable. I was promised a baby at 40 weeks and here I was as big as a house with no baby.

"What can I do to help you, woman?" Caleb said, unsure if his offer would actually help me or hurt him.

"I have walked around the neighborhood, rode the stair master, and eaten spicy food. These are all the things they say to do to go into labor, but nothing is working. There is one more thing they say we can try," I said, calming down a bit.

"And what's that?" Caleb asked, hoping he could help me out.

"They say having sex can start contractions. Do you want to?" I replied, a little embarrassed.

"Sure," Caleb said, taking one for the team.

My bag had been packed for weeks. I had chosen an object for my focal point the Lamaze instructor encouraged I bring. I had two outfits—a pair of stretchy pants and oversized t-shirt if I didn't deflate like I hoped I would and a pair of jeans just in case I went back to normal size. I had a few onesies for Brenna, a new baby blanket and booties, and some mattress-sized pads that I would need if my basement didn't bounce back. (I ended up going home in my stretchy pants and a pad.)

We were living about ten minutes from the hospital, but I was worried that the moment I started having contractions, she would come. My mom told me the story of how I came into the world—contractions for a few minutes, a push or two, and out I came almost before the doctor could get back to the room. Though I was her third child, this would be my luck. So the moment I felt some pain, I was off to the races.

"I'm sorry, but you haven't even started

dilating yet," the doctor sympathized. "Why don't you go back home and try and get some rest. I'm sure it won't be long. You'll want to time your contractions and when they're five minutes apart, go ahead and come back in." And out the door she went.

I was so upset. I was already a week past my due date and I was being sent home. I tried to rationalize that Brenna just felt safe and comfortable inside of me so why would she want to come out? I had created a safe space for her to thrive in and she didn't want to leave my side.

"Come on, woman. Let's head home," Caleb said, as he grabbed my bag.

I've never had good luck in hospitals. I'm so awkward when it comes to 'doing' it right. I work myself up all the time about my ailments and then convince myself I am dying and need to see a doctor. And then as soon as I get into the sterile, white room, I start feeling stupid for even being there. I start talking myself out of needing to be there and plan to leave. This usually happens right when the nurse or doctor walks in. And nine times out of ten, I will have a virus or a negative result and that's that. "Keep an eye on it and come back if it gets worse," they'll say. Or my favorite is, "Just drink plenty of fluids and rest up." I think that's code for "Here's another hypochondriac."

But this night went beyond feeling awkward or stupid. I was disappointed. Though my Brenna was closer to me than she would ever be, I wanted to look into those eyes. I wanted to hold her and rock her to sleep, singing and praying over her. I longed to kiss her chubby cheeks and tickle her tiny feet. I wanted to behold the beauty Caleb and I had made together and dedicate her to the One who made it all possible. I would soon learn even greater disappointment.

Chapter 17

The Promise Appears

I arrived back at the hospital a third time exhausted and in a lot of pain. If I wasn't dilated yet, then I wanted to have a Cesarean. I wasn't going back home without Brenna in my arms.

"You have started to dilate but you're only at a three right now. We're going to give you some Pitocin to try and activate contractions. Your body is already exhausted, and we need you to be able to push when the times comes. It won't be long," the nurse informed us as she left the room.

"The nurse told me out in the hall that they won't give you an epidural until you're at least dilated to a five. They want to make sure it doesn't wear off right when you're in the most pain," Caleb told me, fully engaged in the whole process.

I was so blessed to have Caleb in my life. He was my anchor. He knew how to bring me back down from an emotional high and when to lift me out of a depressive pit. He knew just showing up for me was the most significant evidence and proof of his love for me. And the day our precious daughter would break forth into the world, he was sure to be there every step of the way.

My nurse came back into my room about 20 minutes later to check on my progress. I had finally gotten to five and was ready for my epidural. I had heard about childbirth and the pain that accompanied it but reading about it and experiencing it were two completely different things.

"Are you ready for an epidural, Alora?" she asked with a smile, knowing full well what my answer was. "The anesthesiologist will be in here shortly."

A tall, dark-haired man entered my room with a kit full of supplies. He was clinical, but I wasn't looking for a friend, so I didn't mind. "Ok Alora, I'm going to inject a local anesthetic into the epidural space around your spinal cord. This will block pain signals to your brain, so you won't feel the contractions. When you're fully dilated, the doctor will let you know when it's time to push. You may or may not feel the urge to." And then he began the procedure.

It wasn't long after the injection that I began to feel immense relief. I was even more exhausted and decided to roll onto my side and get some rest. Caleb decided to catch a few z's as well, and tried to get comfortable in the vinyl chair.

"Ow! It hurts so bad! Caleb I can feel everything on this side, but the other side is numb. What's going on?" I screamed unable to keep my composure.

"Let me get the doctor," Caleb frantically replied as he ran out of the room.

"Doctor, my wife is in a lot of pain on one

side. Do you think the epidural has worn off?" Caleb said, trying to be helpful.

"Let me examine her and see what's going on," she said as she put on a new pair of gloves and raced into my room.

"So your husband tells me you're in a lot of pain but only on one side," she said trying to clarify.

"Yes, I fell asleep on my side and rested for a while. Then like a bee sting, I immediately started feeling pain right on this side," I said pointing to my right hip.

"I'm assuming the anesthesiologist didn't tell you that you needed to lay on your back. When you laid on your side, gravity pulled all that liquid down until it all pooled on your left side. That is why you're still numb on your left side. Let me examine you to see how far you're dilated and see if you can get another epidural for the rest of your labor," she said lovingly.

"Okay, you're at eight right now so I will order the epidural for you. This is when you will need it the most," and out the door she left.

"Ouch, this hurts so bad," I groaned, looking to Caleb to take all my pain away. All he could do was just smile at me and hold my hand. But I knew his smile was a cover-up for the concern he had for me. I knew that smile because that was the same look Gwen would give me after I would relapse with bulimia. It was a look of defeat, as if there was nothing anyone could do to help me.

"So I understand you are feeling pain on your right side?" the anesthesiologist asked as he prepared to give me a second epidural.

"Yeah, I can feel every contraction I'm having but the left side is completely numb. I guess I shouldn't have laid on my side," I said, almost apologetic.

"Go ahead and sit up. I'm going to remove the needle from your back and insert another one," he said and with that he ripped the tape off my back in one swoosh. It felt as if I was being scourged. I couldn't decide what was worse, this assault or the contractions I was trying desperately to be numb to. Caleb was livid with his insensitivity and lack of compassion. Large tears welled up in my eyes and as if in slow motion, inched their way down my cheeks.

After three tries of inserting the needle into my spine, it made contact and I was beginning to "feel" the pain subside. However, at this point I felt immense pressure to push. He kept telling me not to push because it wasn't time for that. But how can you stop gravity? How can you tell an excited dog when he sees his owner to not tinkle? Or to tell a baby to just stop crying? Somehow, I managed to resist the push and once the anesthesia settled in, I couldn't feel a thing. I made sure I remained flat on my back and just waited to dilate to ten.

By the time Brenna came into this world, I had been in labor for 30 hours. I was exhausted and emotionally spent. Once she was placed in my arms, I vowed I would never let her go. She was so precious. Dark wavy hair tickled my face as I snuggled up to her. She instantly took to nursing and before you knew it, we were both fading into dreamland.

Complications

"Caleb!" I screamed. "My head hurts so bad. I feel like it's going to explode," I shrieked. "I can't even lift up my head without excruciating pain. Please get the doctor," I said in between sobs.

"Doctor," Caleb cried, "please help my wife."

"What's going on, Alora?" the doctor responded as she began to examine me.

"It's my head. It hurts so bad. I can't lift it up without it killing me." I said, begging for the pain to go away. At this point, Caleb had to take Brenna from me. I couldn't even hold her.

"This is rare, 1 in 100, but I think you have a spinal headache," my doctor concluded. She continued, "It most likely was caused after your second epidural. I heard you were poked a few times."

"So what is a spinal headache and how does it go away?" I asked, trying to focus on her words as much as I could.

"It's a leakage of spinal fluid through a puncture hole in the tough membrane that surrounds the spinal cord. This leakage decreases the pressure exerted by the spinal fluid on the brain and spinal cord, which leads to a headache. If left untreated, it could result in a subdural hematoma or a seizure."

She continued, "It's good it happened while you're still here. What I advise is an epidural blood patch. Essentially, we draw blood from your arm and insert it directly into the puncture holes in your spine. The blood will coagulate which will restore the spinal fluid pressure. After this procedure, you'll need to lay flat on your back for four hours for it to work."

"Whatever you need to do to relieve this pain. I can't even think clearly." I replied, understanding about a quarter of what she just said. All the while Caleb was beyond livid with the anesthesiologist for his shoddy work—everything from not telling me I had to lay flat on my back to ripping off the tape from my back to now putting me at risk for a brain bleed.

I looked over at Caleb and was met again with that concerned smile. "It's going to be okay, Babe. Just make sure our baby is taken care of," I advised.

Finally, I was back to feeling better and could hold Brenna again. I wondered if those five hours I lost with Brenna would affect her ability to bond with me. I couldn't help but think about my entry into this world and the lack of connection my mother had with me after the bombshell my father laid on her. The one thing I wanted—to never let her go—was being forced on me. I would later find myself wrestling with the same desire and the same outcome.

Chapter 18

Winging It

I was a mom and I was overcome with emotions and fears. This tiny infant was my responsibility. I had experience raising children when I worked as a nanny, but Lena was already one year old when I started. I was the youngest in my family and my nieces and nephews always lived far away from me. My best friend didn't have children. So here I was, winging it. How did I not take the time to study the days and weeks after the birth? I was so worried about getting through pregnancy and then labor that I failed to read up on life after the help, phone calls, and baked lasagna were gone. Caleb would be going back to work that following Monday and it would just be me and Brenna; and Brenna would tell me what she wanted not in words but rather in screams.

What in the world is wrong with my baby? Brenna was in so much pain. She would scream and toss and turn. I didn't know what was wrong, therefore, I didn't know how to help her. I called her pediatrician and took her in. "Your baby has colic. Simply stated, Brenna will cry for no reason, for long periods of time, and because of that air will sometimes get trapped in her tummy. The colic increases the likelihood of gas and constipation because of all the trapped air," her doctor calmly stated, making me feel a lot better. "There are things you can do to help her when she begins to cry. And there are foods to avoid while you're nursing to decreases the chances of colic." And that was it. I left the doctor's office relieved but ready for a new challenge.

Brenna was my pride and joy. I never knew this kind of love or connection. Even with all the crying, I couldn't believe how blessed I was. Brenna was a combination of Caleb and myself. She had my pug nose and Caleb's eyebrows. She had big blue eyes and lots of hair. She was sweet and curious and independent from an early age. She had her own agenda. She walked early, was potty trained early, began reading early, and before I knew it, she was in kindergarten. She would put on her purple backpack and her light-up tennis shoes, I'd throw her long blonde hair into pigtails, and off we'd go to school.

Watching Brenna grow up before my eyes was truly a difficult process. It was like trying to catch the wind. I wanted to grab time and command it to stand still. Instead, time seemed to go by at warp speed. I never thought I'd love anyone else as much as Brenna, until Shiloh came along!

The Loss

I miscarried shortly after I had Brenna. Caleb and I were on a church camping trip. I was ten weeks pregnant and had actually started telling people. We were ecstatic. We knew we wanted our kids close in age so they could grow up together. Our dream was that they would be best friends their whole lives. But that first night sleeping in the back of our Suburban, I woke up in the middle of the night. My bladder was full so I quietly got out of the truck and started walking to the bathrooms.

I felt something running down my legs but I knew it wasn't urine. I had my flashlight with me so I lit the ground behind me where I saw trail of blood following me. I knew my baby was in danger. I got to the bathroom and as I relieved myself, I saw it. My baby didn't make it. I hadn't known about miscarriage. That was not a conversation I had ever had with anyone. But I knew what was floating in the toilet was the result of a miscarriage. I was numb. There was no emotion, almost an insensitive response to what just occurred.

I walked back to the truck following the blood trail with my eyes. "Caleb, I think I just miscarried," I said with the same emotion as telling him what I had for lunch the day prior.

"Oh my gosh. What happened?" he replied with more emotion than I had ever seen before.

I told him and he rushed me to the hospital. I remember looking out the window as numb as can be. Though I didn't know at the time that I was numb. I didn't think it was a big deal. It was like I was having my period. The blood didn't shock me. The loss didn't move me, but it sure affected Caleb. Though he didn't at the time share with me all his emotions, I knew this loss hurt him. Later I learned this was traumatic for him. He felt confused, bewildered, and sad. And though I was numb, I knew I wasn't responding normally. I wanted to feel, but like trying to catch the wind, I just couldn't.

Life went back to normal. I went back to work, Brenna went to daycare, Caleb went back to work. And before too long I was pregnant again. I was excited. Caleb, on the other hand, was cautious. He didn't want to go through another loss. We had just moved to Atwater, Oklahoma. Caleb had been climbing the corporate ladder and was offered a manager role at a call center. It had good benefits and more pay. It didn't take us too long to jump at the chance for a better life. But this meant leaving my friends and family in California. The only highlight besides the salary was my sister, Lauren, and her family who lived 30 minutes away in Redfield. She had a five-year-old daughter, Carly. I never grew up with my cousins so I was excited for Brenna to have a cousin to play with.

Lauren was like a drug to me. I grew to need her but she wasn't good for me. Her approval was something I strived for but never received. I was always thought of as the little sister or even her daughter she was forced to raise. She had to grow up fast. She was only two-and-a-half years older than I but she seemed much older. Since Mom and Dad both worked full time, we were left to fend for ourselves—walk to school, walk home from school, do our homework, and wait for someone older than 12 to arrive home to tuck us into bed. Because Diane had it out for me, Lauren stepped into a protector role. She knew how to handle Diane. And so my loyalty towards Lauren began at an early age.

Though Lauren was the reason for my relapse five years prior, I still needed her. She never apologized for that comment, probably because I didn't let her know how much it hurt me. I never knew how to express my emotions. They were better off bottled up. I figured Lauren was all I had. I didn't want to risk losing her, even if she was toxic.

The Unthinkable

I sat in the lobby at Pre-Paid Legal waiting to be called back in for an interview. We were settled in Atwater, Oklahoma. Brenna was all of five months old and doing well at the close-by daycare we had found. And even though we found out I was expecting a month earlier, I figured I could work up until my due date when an old familiar feeling began. "I couldn't be again," I thought. "Surely God wouldn't put me and Caleb through this a second time."

"Alora Stone," an enthusiastic secretary called. "Are you Alora?" she continued, staring right at me.

"Oh, yes," I quickly replied. I stood up, shook her hand, and began to follow her down the hallway pulling my sweater down as far as it would go.

"Ok, you can go right in and have a seat. Maria will be with you in a minute." Then she turned away and walked out.

My eyes got big. I reached behind me to see if I could feel anything wet. "Oh my God!" I panicked. "It couldn't be. It can't be!" I said beneath my breath. Quickly I reached into my purse for a tissue. Just then Maria walked in.

"You must be Alora. I'm Maria. It's nice to meet you," she began, sounding so nice. "So tell me, what made you apply to work here?"

How could I continue. I'm in the middle of what could only be another miscarriage. My mind was so anxious. How can I focus on answering job interview questions? Does my face reveal the panic that is happening on the inside? All of these questions raced through my mind as I responded, "I have experience in data entry and it seems like something I would be good at," I instinctively replied hoping that short answer was sufficient.

"Do you know much about Pre-Paid Legal?" she continued. I guess my answer was good enough for round two. I nodded no. She then went into a five-minute dissertation of the company, how it was founded, and how it's grown to be a multi-million dollar company that seeks to provide a low rate for legal services at your fingertips. I had to admit I struggled staying focused. I occasionally nodded in agreement or said "really" inquisitively. After a few more questions, the interview was over.

"Ok, I'll be in touch. It was nice to meet you, Alora," she said, as she walked me back to the waiting room. I tried to stay right behind her as long as possible for fear of her seeing my backside.

I made my way to the bathroom before heading out. I was bloody. This couldn't be good. I needed to get to the hospital right away. I headed home to talk with Caleb about it. It was a Saturday and my doctor's office wasn't open so he rushed me to the emergency room. I could only imagine what was going on in his mind. He was quiet on the way to the hospital. I knew he had to be processing this. I wouldn't know how he truly felt for years. He probably didn't know either.

"Can you please help my wife?" Caleb said almost fearful in tone. "We think she miscarried." He sounded resolute. That didn't make me feel good. Caleb was the positive one of the two of us, He was the glass-is-half-full kind of guy. His defeated posture concerned me. No longer was I only worried about the baby but now I was worried about my husband.

I was taken back right away. A nurse came in with an ultrasound machine to check me out. Holding Caleb's hand, we prayed to ourselves that somehow there was a mistake and this blood could be explained. I didn't realize it until the nurse asked me how far along I was but I was at the ten-week mark. My heart dropped. This was how far I was along when I last miscarried.

"There's your baby!" she said, exhaling a sigh of relief. I'm sure she had been in these kinds of situations where the outcomes weren't as positive. Today she was able to give us relief. We both exhaled as if we had been holding our breath for the last hour. "Thank you so much," we both said at the same time.

"Just make sure you see your regular doctor on Monday," she mandated as she left the room. We both let out the biggest thank you to God, then left the hospital, not sure what actually happened. But it didn't matter. Our baby was alive and that's all that mattered.

Another close call. I thought about my angel

again. I wondered if God had him pulling family duty now. Was he assigned to me and my little family or did I have more angels watching over us? As we headed back home, I sat looking out the car window smiling at the thought to my question.

I called my doctor's office first thing Monday morning. I told them what had occurred over the weekend and she got me right in. Caleb was back to work so I went to my appointment by myself. I figured it would be a good visit. I'd get to hear my baby's heartbeat again and see my little pea on the screen. I was looking forward to getting a green light that all was well. But that's not exactly what happened. "What? How is that possible?" I said, utterly confused.

"It's called vanishing twin syndrome. It typically happens in the first trimester. Some women don't even know they've miscarried because the symptoms don't always involve vaginal bleeding. The only way we can know for sure that you miscarried a twin is the empty sac," she said, as she pointed to the monitor. "See, this sac is empty and this sac has your healthy baby in it."

"Wow, I didn't even know I was carrying twins. So where did the baby go? Last time I actually passed my baby in the toilet," I questioned. I was so numb. I was so confused.

My doctor began to explain that most often the tissue of the baby gets reabsorbed into the mom's body over time. She said there was no way to know if my baby was a boy or a girl but because they were in different sacs the twins would've been fraternal. I wondered if this would affect my baby as she grew up. Even though I was only ten-weeks along, I knew how twins create a bond in vitro.

    I took more of an interest in caring for myself. I didn't want to chance any more complications so I would take walks every day with Brenna in her stroller. I would have to bundle her up because fall was beginning to turn into winter. Brenna was still a baby so she didn't really know what was to come but we knew she would be excited when her baby sister would come in May. By then she would be 15-months old. We dreamed of our girls being best friends and growing up enjoying each phase of life together. We would soon learn that the girls had a love-hate relationship with each other growing up. And this would bring a lot of fear and pain into my life.

Chapter 19

On The Move

Caleb and I both had on-again, off-again relationships with our sisters. Caleb's sister, Sarah, lived in Washington state. They were just a year apart but they were never best friends. They were raised in the same home with the same parents but had different perspectives of how life was as a child. It wasn't until they got a lot older that they started seeing each other's viewpoint of how life was for the other. Now they get along really well.

"I quit my job today," Caleb said one day in January. I knew he wasn't happy at his job but I thought we'd have a conversation about it first. This was the job that moved us to Oklahoma just six months earlier. "I just can't work for someone who has zero integrity," he continued before I got a word out of my mouth. "I hope you're not mad," he said with finality.

"Caleb, I'm six months pregnant. What are we going to do for health insurance?" I said, starting to panic. I had always worried about money and the worry was legitimate. Earlier that year, we pawned a VCR in order to buy diapers. We were struggling financially since I decided not to work after the vanishing twin. I was staying home with Brenna and though Caleb was a manager, he wasn't making that much.

"I was thinking we could call Dad and Judith and see if we could live with them temporarily until we land on our feet. I know they would love to see Brenna," he replied.

Caleb and I had only been together for six months when we got married. We both were living in North Dakota so I didn't know his family. In fact, our honeymoon was spent in Seattle visiting his family the summer after we got married. I had only been around his family a few times when he proposed this, but what choice did we have? I was not going back to North Dakota.

"Ok, make the call," I responded, praying this decision wouldn't come back to haunt us.

Caleb's dad, Steve, and stepmom Judith, lived in a two-bedroom farmhouse 60 miles north of Seattle. The three of us would spend the next three months living in a ten-by-twelve bedroom and then one month more after our new baby was born. Though it was small, we loved living there. They both welcomed us and provided for us until we could get our feet on the ground. The first thing we did was get me on state insurance. I was six-months pregnant and due for another check up in a few weeks. I needed insurance and a doctor!

As I look back on that year, I knew God was watching over us. We never went hungry or were homeless. We always had enough, even though at times it was a struggle. But as I thought about our life starting over again, I felt at peace.

God would not leave us and that's all I needed to remember to keep going. Brenna was excited to be at Grandma's and Grandpa's house. She loved being the center of attention and that's exactly what happened. Caleb's sister had a six-year old daughter, Sophia, who loved Brenna. She would act like Brenna was her doll. They got along really well. I sat back and sighed, "This will be good."

Hold On

"Caleb, I'm having contractions!" I anxiously said raising my voice. How could this be? I thought. I'm only seven months along.

We were in Seattle for the night enjoying our second anniversary while Caleb's parents were babysitting Brenna. We made our way to the hospital in downtown Seattle. My contractions were five minutes apart. I was rushed in and hooked up to a monitor. I was given a shot to help Shiloh's lungs develop if she would end up coming early. And I was given a drug to stop my contractions. Then we waited.

At this point, prayer was a regular activity but in the past few months, I had increased my conversations with, rather my pleas to God. My body had gone through so much in the last year. Ever since the first miscarriage, my body seemed to be fighting against me. The only one who could give me peace was God, so I ran into his arms. My contractions ceased. I was so tired and by the time we got back to the hotel, it was 6:00 a.m. The whole point in going away was to get rest. Now we were more tired than when we left for Seattle, but Shiloh was safe and that's all that mattered.

Ironically, Shiloh decided to stay an extra

week in my belly before she decided to make her appearance. And her lungs? Well, they were overly developed. When she cried, our ears bled.

Shiloh would not take a bottle. She would not take a pacifier. And she would not go to anybody else. She was attached to my hip. It was good I had decided to stay at home with the girls, although I'm sure she would've had to bite the bullet and take a bottle if she was hungry enough. But Mama was there night and day and Shiloh knew she had me wrapped around her little finger.

Goodbye Tour

From the day I told Caleb about ED in 1998 until 2006, I had gone cold turkey with no more purging. Caleb's words "I can't be with anyone who harms themselves like that" kept me going all those years. I couldn't risk losing him. He was the best thing that had ever happened to me. I continued being fearful of food and gaining weight. But the line would be crossed only when I stuck my fingers down my throat. Everything else would be in my head. That was until tragedy hit.

"Dad and I are going to taking a road trip to visit the family. First we'll drive up California to visit Grandma and all the extended family, then we'll come see you guys in Washington," Mom told me one day. (Lauren had already moved back to North Dakota to be close to Dad because he was battling cancer again.) I knew Dad wasn't doing very good with his health. He had battled cancer for so many years and I knew he had just been diagnosed with lung cancer.

"Is Dad feeling better?" I asked quite confused.

"No, he's actually dying, Alora. This will be his final trip to say goodbye to the family. He loves you all so much," Mom responded, trying to hold back the gulp in her throat.

There were no words. What do you say to that? All I could muster up the courage to say it would be wonderful to see them both.

The day came. He was so exhausted and felt terrible. We spent a few times that week in the ER getting his lungs drained. He was on borrowed time. The kids were five and six. They had no idea how ill Grandpa was so they kept jumping on him and asking him to play with them. It broke my heart. Dad was such a good sport. He did all he could to make those four days special for us.

On the last day, we laid in the same bed and had a conversation. "Is there anything we need to talk about, Alora?" Dad said, wanting to make atonement for anything that needed atoning for. "I love you so much. Take care of Mom," he said with tears streaming down his cheeks.

The dam broke and all I could do was just tell him how proud I was of him and how much I loved him too. There was nothing left to say. We were good. It was such a special gift he gave me. A few short weeks later, he died.

Shortly after the funeral, I lost it. I was so angry at God. Dad and I had just started getting close after all these years of growing up with an absentee dad. And then God took him. I couldn't hold ED back. He always seemed to battle for my soul whenever I would be upset at God. He met me in my pain and promised me relief. After seven years, I relapsed. I found myself puking seven years of heartbreak, loss, and anger up. Everything had been bottled up. After I flushed the toilet and cleaned up, fear flooded in. "What have I done?" I screamed under my breath.

Would Caleb leave me? Would this betrayal be too much for him to bear? I was paralyzed. I couldn't tell him but I couldn't not tell him either. I was so scared. It was my decision to bring ED back into our lives. It was like I cheated on Caleb with ED. How in the world would he ever be able to trust me again? All these questions and more rattled around in my head. There would be no right time to tell him. I just needed to and I knew it would be better if I told him sooner than later.

I remembered this kind of fear. It was 15 years prior when I was forced to tell Mom about bulimia. The fear lied in how she would respond, and now it lied in how Caleb would respond. I knew this wasn't going to end the same way it did with Mom telling me to just not do it again. I knew Caleb would want me to get help. And that was something I was scared to do, not so much getting help but figuring out how to overcome this beast. I had tried in the past but it always met me in my weakness. And this was no different.

"I have to tell you something, Caleb." I trembled, starting to feel sick to my stomach.

"What is it, Alora? Are you ok?" he replied sounding so concerned.

And then the tears started to well up. I couldn't hold them in any longer. Coming over to me and putting his arm around me, he asked what was wrong. Before I knew it I was confessing what I had done. This took him by surprise.

He didn't know much about ED. I made sure to keep everything hidden. I didn't share with Caleb about my internal struggles. So this seemed to be completely out of the blue. But I knew it was just a matter of time with Dad passing.

Though he was floored and confused, he was there for me. He said we'd get through it together. He was loving and supportive. I realized that day that I hadn't done any work with ED in seven years. I had just kept him hidden from the world. It would take another decade for me to have the strength and the tools to say goodbye to ED for good.

Chapter 20

The Call

I told Caleb when we were dating that I was glad he was no longer in the military and that he wasn't in the ministry. I wanted a regular life. I felt like I had lived in a fishbowl for too long. Though my relationship with God had gotten a lot better since Dad had become a minister, I still didn't want to be in ministry. And I had heard about how military guys cheated on their spouses all the time. So I was content I had a husband in the business industry.

"Alora, do you mind taking the girls to the mall. I want to fast and pray about something and I want to be alone," Caleb said one day when the girls were toddlers.

"Of course. I'll be home for dinner," I said, having no idea what he could possibly asking God about.

Caleb has since become very open with his feelings but back then he rarely opened up. I truly had no idea what it could be about, but I took the girls to the mall and let them play. I had been a stay-at-home mom for the past few years but there was no staying at home. I'd take them everywhere. We'd go to the library, zoo, shopping, parks, and anywhere we could find sunshine or play. One of our favorite places was TubeTime, an indoor playground with tubes, slides, ball pits, and trampolines. I loved our times together.

"I have to tell you something, Alora," Caleb said when we got home. I was a little nervous because he sounded real official.

"What is it?" I said trying to act calm.

"I felt like God was calling me into the ministry and I wanted to fast and pray and seek Him. I ended up asking Him if He wanted me to go into the ministry and He verbally said 'yes!'"

"That's great, Babe!" I said in excitement.

"But I thought you didn't want me to go into the ministry or the military?" He said feeling relieved.

"That was years ago. I trust God more now. And I want to do what He wants us to do. If He is calling you into the ministry, then who am I to stop you?" I said, with a sigh of relief that it wasn't another move. At that point we had moved so many times and I was so over it. Only God knew we'd be moving a half dozen more times before finally settling down.

"So what is the next step?" I continued.

"I guess I need to find a school to attend and go from there," he casually replied.

Caleb had been a Christian for three years and God was calling him into the ministry. I couldn't help but think of the way God had called Dad decades earlier. God has a way of calling the unlearned and unsuspecting folk to preach His word.

Caleb found a seminary in Portland, Oregon to attend, which was three hours away. He would leave on a Thursday morning, be in class on Thursday and Friday, and drive home Friday night. He continued to work as a manager and be a dad to Brenna and Shiloh. We knew God was providing energy, money, and resources. If God was calling him into this, He would provide a way for it to happen. Of course, it took a lot of faith and trust to believe He would provide. Our faith was still growing.

After Caleb had been in school for five years, he was finally getting ready to graduate. We were all so proud of him. Midway through his schooling, we had made the decision to move to Spokane where I had gone back to work after the girls started school. At that point, Caleb could no longer work full-time and carry his school load. These classes were 400 level and above. He went to part-time and I transferred jobs to go to full-time. He would fly to Portland once a week for class. He was working as an associate pastor for a local church and was looking forward to getting his diploma and closing the chapter on school and travel.

Looking back now, I don't see how we managed—school, work, kids, travel, ministry, and keeping the house in order. At this point, the girls really got along. We had them enrolled in an after school program called Big Brothers Big Sisters of America, which was a lot of fun for them. They would have tutors available to help the kids with homework. They would provide a snack and lots of activities. Depending on the day, either Caleb or I would pick them up. They also had some summer day camps that helped us out as well.

Caleb was also serving at Youth for Christ once a week. He loved being involved in community service. He knew that is where your faith met the real world. He served middle-school and high-schoolers. Some stories Caleb would share with me were so sad. So many juveniles were left to fend for themselves, some coming from abusive households. It was always an opportunity to share the love of Jesus with those kids who might not ever hear about God. Caleb had a heart for the lost and for the underdog. God had sure changed him when he gave his life to the Lord. I was seeing transformation happen right before my eyes.

Move To The Beach

Caleb finished his time at the Youth for Christ and the church and was ready to look for a lead pastor role. He answered a posting for a church in Western Washington right next to the beach and a few months later we were packing up the U-Haul again. This time we'd be moving to a quaint tourist town, population 900. It was bigger than the town I lived in when Dad pastored, but not by much. The nearest grocery store was 45 minutes away unless you counted the convenient store ten miles away. The kids loved how close it was to the beach. We rented a vacation home a few blocks from the beach's entrance and settled in.

The kids were in third and fourth grade by this time. The school was small so they combined grades which meant the girls were in the same class. They made friends pretty quickly and got involved. Shiloh started swim lessons and Brenna started gymnastics. I loved being able to provide outlets for the girls. They were growing up so fast.

With every move, we dreamt of it being our last one. We had moved so many times by this point and it was always to get ahead. I didn't know when enough would be enough. We had always lived paycheck to paycheck growing up and now I found myself living the same kind of life with my family. I was tired of the struggle but knew one of these days, the struggle would end. Caleb began preaching and getting settled in when odd things began to surface.

"Hi, Pastor Caleb. Do you have a minute?" asked one of the elders who stopped by the house one day. The church didn't have an office for him so Caleb made one of the rooms in the house an office.

"Sure, come on in. Would you like some coffee?" Caleb replied, not sure what he'd bring up.

"I have a letter here that I've written up. It includes 10 items that I need you to sign saying you agree to the terms," he casually said, taking out the letter from his back pocket. "I will not include my past 'chasing skirts' in my testimony. I promise not to sue the church."

"What is this all about?" Caleb asked very confused.

"Well, I think it's best that you agree to some of the things that could pose a problem in the future," he said, acting as if this was normal.

This was early on in Caleb's ministry there and the situation got even more weird. We had no idea what we had gotten ourselves into. Later on Caleb would learn the elders lied about how the previous pastor died. They said he died of cancer but in reality he had invited his entire family over for Easter weekend and the morning of Easter he went out behind the house and shot himself in the head. Now we had a church who had not healed wanting Caleb to walk like him, talk like him, preach like him, and be about the things the previous pastor was. This was too much for Caleb to take. It was not healthy and before we knew it, Caleb was asked to leave after only nine months.

Was this really what God had called us to? Did we impulsively say yes to this church without inquiring of the Lord? Did we overlook obvious red flags? Did we get distracted by the water's edge and living in a beach town? We had nowhere to go. How can this be happening to us? But staying was not an option on the table. They wanted Caleb out since he didn't play by their rules.

Back On The Road

The girls had to say goodbye to their new friends again. I worried about how this would affect them as they got older. I knew moving around a lot as a child affected me, but at this point, we didn't have a choice. Caleb suggested we move to Portland, the location of his seminary. He had connections there and hoped he'd land a job quickly. Because of the one year employment contract Caleb had with the church at the beach, they had to pay him out. His salary for three months allowed us to pay for six months of rent at our new apartment. I quickly found a job at a bank as a teller but Caleb was unable to find anything.

The girls were so good about falling forward. It wouldn't be until they got older that they would struggle with anxiety. As soon as we moved into the apartment in Portland, the girls made friends with a neighbor. They were sisters and the same age as the girls. We had just gotten a puppy the year before and they had a dog too. The kids decided to start a dog walking and pet care business. They made up flyers for their services and handed it out in the apartment complex. I smiled to myself because the kids seemed to be thriving in our new move, but we, unfortunately, didn't have a plan. Time was running out. Caleb was receiving unemployment benefits but no job. This was the beginning of 2009 when a recession was affecting many Americans. But I seemed to be doing well at the bank, which would keep us afloat for a little while. We just had to hang on a little bit longer.

I had to ride the subway to get to work in the city, since we were living in a suburb outside of Portland and my job was downtown. I would have to get up at 5:30 a.m. to get ready, drive to the subway, take a 30-minute ride, and then walk eight blocks to the bank. I was still in my 90-day probationary period when I was called into the main conference room one morning. I hadn't even gotten my coat off when I was ushered in to take a seat. As soon as I walked in, my eyes met a room full of suits. There was my manager, my supervisor, the head teller, the market manager, and the regional manager all sitting there staring at me.

"Alora, the reason we've called you in today

is because you did something that goes outside the boundaries of our ethical standards," my boss sternly said.

"I don't understand," I said. "What did I do?" I sheepishly asked.

They went on to explain I had altered a transaction the day before. One of the deposits I had processed had a check that wasn't signed. I thought the check would come back and subtract itself from the original deposit amount leaving the customer negative. Since she had gotten cash back, I had her signature. So I cut her signature off from the deposit slip and taped it to a new deposit ticket that had the amount on it minus that unsigned check. I truly thought I was helping the customer. I had even asked my supervisor if that was okay to do and she said yes. However, she didn't speak up at the meeting. She just sat there, quiet as could be.

Why didn't I speak up? I had been told it was okay to do it like that by a supervisor and now I was getting fired over it. But I was too scared to open my mouth. I just took it. I let them fire me. I let them have their security guards escort me down into the break room to get my belongings out of my locker, then usher me out the front doors like a criminal.

It was raining. It was like God was crying with me. That day I had driven to work, or at least Portland. The parking garage was a mile away. I walked in the rain defeated and scared to death. Now both Caleb and I were unemployed. We were running out of time and money and now another decision was being made for us. I couldn't believe what was happening. The kids had already been in two schools that year. Another move would require them to transfer a third time. Where could we go? We found ourselves in a similar predicament a decade earlier but this time we'd be traveling east towards Mom's home—back to a family that had wrecked me before. I was hoping a decade would've been enough time to change.

Chapter 21

The Earthquake

We pulled into Ridgefield, West Virginia in February of 2010. Brenna had just turned ten years old and Shiloh was trailing behind her at nine. We were greeted with lots of family. My mother, along with my sister, Diane and her kids, Cassie and Simon. The last time I had seen my sister was at Dad's funeral four years earlier. We were both cordial. At this point, time had seemed to mend fences. We were on a talking basis but pretty casual. I had learned not to get close. We'd exchange Christmas cards and Facebook messages. Occasionally we'd talk on the phone but those calls were few and far between. For us, that was what being on good terms looked like. However, things always seemed to go south anytime we'd be in the same room. I was back to looking over my shoulder.

Lauren was living her own life in Montana. She was divorced from Sam and was with a new man. They had been together for five years and had just had a daughter. She was thinking any day he would be proposing, but that wouldn't be the case. In fact, it was the opposite. He came home one day and told Lauren he didn't know if he loved her and wanted to break up. She was devastated since she had moved to Montana to be with him. She didn't have family there, so he was her life. Carly was 16 years old. Before too long Lauren would call West Virginia her new home.

Lauren and I got along well, though she could be rude and cutting. I knew it was just her personality. I tried not to take things too personally. By then, she had confided in me about all her relationships and I with her. She seemed to love my family and I was looking forward to her moving to West Virginia. It would be the first time we'd all live in the same place since we were children. Carly adored her cousins, and my girls loved Tessa, the newest addition to the family. She wasn't even one when they moved. It seemed like Mom had finally gotten her wish that all her children would get along.

The girls settled into their third school for the year. They were still able to fall forward and maintain resiliency. Shiloh started cheerleading and Brenna made the volleyball team while Caleb and I got management jobs at Kmart. We had just moved into our own place after staying with mom for nine months. We had landed on our feet and felt so taken care of. God had walked this path with us and never left us. Though at times in my life I felt alone, I knew I wasn't any longer. I had family again. I was elated.

"Alora, I think your sister is on the phone. She says you waited on her today and was very rude. She's saying she's a customer, not your sister," my boss said almost sad for me.

No, this can't be happening again, I thought to myself.

"I'll get back on the phone and ask her to tell me the story again so I can write it down. You listen in and see if it's your sister," she continued.

"Hi, thank you for waiting. Ok, I have something to write with. Can you please tell me again what happened so I can write it down?" my boss asked, acting like a detective.

"Oh yes, I came to the pharmacy today to purchase some items and your cashier, Alora, treated me horribly," Diane said.

I couldn't help myself. All those years of her hate and betrayal boiled up in me and had nowhere else to go. "Why are you ruining my life!" I screamed at Diane. "This is Alora. Why are you doing this?" I continued.

The next thing I heard was a dial tone. I was upset, shaking and crying. I walked out of the store to catch my breath. I had no idea what had preceded that phone call, but it would send division through the family that would last longer than a decade.

"Caleb, I just got off the phone with Diane. She pretended to be a customer and say I was really rude to her. She tried to get me fired! This is so low. I can't even think right now," I said, barely able to get the words out.

It was a summer day and the girls were home. Carly had spent the night. They knew to go over to Grandma's house across the street when they woke up. I would soon find out that Diane had come into our house uninvited and awakened Shiloh. My mom owned a daycare business, and that day they were going to take the kids to the pool but one of the kids forgot to bring a swimsuit. So Diane decided to ask Shiloh if she had one she could borrow. But instead of waiting for Shiloh to come over that morning, she barged into our home, woke up my children, and asked for something she didn't need until after lunchtime.

Shiloh spoke her mind. She was fearless to express herself and that morning was no different. She told Diane no and asked her why she was in her house. This infuriated Diane. A switch flipped in her mind. "You don't talk to your elders like that. I'm your aunt and I deserve respect," she shot back.

I think this is when Diane decided to call my work, wanting to destroy my family. She couldn't help herself. If she was disrespected, she would lash out. Just then Brenna walked over to Grandma's house to see if she needed help with anything. She had decided the night before to do something nice for Grandma. As soon as she walked in, Diane asked her to come into the back office. She then began to yell at her and throw magazines at her. She cussed her out and locked her in the room.

In her delusion, Diane got my kids mixed up and thought that was Shiloh. She had lost her mind. The office had a back door so Brenna ran out and went back home. She was crying and told Shiloh and Carly all about what had just taken place. Without missing a beat, Shiloh stormed outside to confront Diane. My little ten year old was going up against the boogeyman.

"Why did you come into our house and wake us up for something you didn't need for hours later? And then why did you lock Brenna in a room after throwing books at her and cussing at her?" Shiloh calmly asked.

"Let's take this outside," Diane barked back.

They walked outside to the front porch. Diane continued, "How dare you come to my place of work and disrespect me. I will sue you for everything you have," she screamed.

She was threatening to sue my ten-year old daughter? I couldn't believe the story when I heard it later that day, but nothing that occurred had seemed real that day. Everything blew my mind. My sister had lost it, walking into someone else's home uninvited, yelling and cursing at her niece who did nothing to her, calling my work to try to have me fired, then telling my child she was going to sue her. Yes, she had officially lost her mind.

The girls called me shortly after Shiloh's talk with Diane to tell me what was going on. I was in shock. I called Caleb to tell him everything that had just occurred. He marched right over to Mom's house to confront Diane. All along my mother just kept saying, 'Come on, Diane.' There were kids in Mom's daycare but Diane didn't care. She and Caleb went at it, curse words flying out of both of their mouths. Diane even denied calling my place of work. "So if I hit redial on this phone it won't call Kmart?" Caleb quickly fired back. "It shouldn't," Diane said smug.

That day was the straw that broke the camel's back. Caleb left madder than he ever was before. We had only been in West Virginia for a year and a half and already there were problems. Would we have to move again? I was so worried for all of us. Only time would tell how the dust would settle.

Mom had witnessed Diane's behavior first-hand. She had all the details of what she did to her granddaughters earlier that day and still she supported Diane. It was like my childhood all over again. Diane was a master manipulator. And Mom was co-dependent with Diane. The only thing that would ever happen to Diane was a slap on the wrist. 'But mainly it was our duty to look past the things Diane had done. She would always say, "That's just Diane," as if she was incapable of change and shouldn't be held responsible for anything. It was so damaging as a little girl not having someone have my back. And that never changed.

I thought for sure I would have the support of Lauren. We were close. I thought we were friends. "Lauren, can you please speak up for me to Mom?" I pleaded with Lauren. What she replied would hit me like a pile of bricks. It was the same feeling I had when she told me I was the fat one 15 years earlier.

"I have my own problems. You and Diane have been fighting since you were kids. Figure it out," she responded.

At that moment, I knew it was me and my family against the world. There were so many people who had either rejected us or attacked us. We had been attacked from every corner and then it was our children's turn to be in the line of fire. I was terrified because I couldn't protect my children. The darkness of the world that once only hit Caleb and me was now casting a shadow on them.

Chapter 22

The Talk Begins

I had a lot of questions—questions I couldn't answer. And the first one was why I was having a nightly battle in my mind. I would have two constant dreams. One was evil and one was good. In the same night I would be chased through an apartment complex by the boogeyman and the next scene I would be held by God Himself as I fell off the cliff, waking up before hitting the water. I knew I needed to go back into therapy, having gone shortly after my father died and it was truly helpful. What could it hurt?

At that point in my life, I was not taking any meds. I had been prescribed an anti-depressant years earlier, and I had felt so much better. But life had thrown me a curveball and I found I was struggling once more. We had moved again, this time to a suburb in Millhaven, Ohio where Caleb was pastoring a church in a distressed area. By this time, the girls were teenagers. Shiloh was finishing out middle school and Brenna started high school. I couldn't believe my girls were the same age I was when ED got my attention.

I prayed, begged, and pleaded with God to keep them safe from ED.

"Hi, my name is Victoria. It's nice to meet you, Alora," my new therapist started.

She was pretty, with medium dark hair that had been put into a ponytail. She wore denim and red high heels. She wore bright red lipstick. Most people would look like they were trying too hard, but not Victoria. This was her style that only she could pull off. Right away I felt intimidated.

One thing I had always struggled with was comparing myself to others. *Am I prettier than she is? Am I thinner? Do I sing better than her? Are my kids better behaved than those kids?* I did this constantly, from how nice a woman smelled to the glasses she wore. *Where did I fit in? Was I better or worse?* That was the only question I would ask myself. To me this pattern of behavior was all I knew. Where did it come from? How can one's esteem be left up to who is wearing a better fragrance? And the comparisons were just getting worse.

"Hi, it's nice to meet you too," I said sheepishly.

"So tell me what brings you in today?" she said, glancing over my file. She had my intake form in my file that would eventually be filled with stories of pain and fear.

"My eating disorder is back," I said quietly, feeling a lot of shame.

What did that even mean? Did ED ever really leave me? Or did I just mean that I had been able to push him to the corners of my life but now he barged in and took over? Did it mean that I had gone back to the act of purging? Or did he just have overwhelming power over me that I feared for my life?

I had seen a few therapists in the same practice before Victoria but we never clicked. You need to be able to trust your therapist and my first one going back into therapy had made me feel paranoid.

"Come in and have a seat," she had said, motioning me to the couch.

Right away I scanned the room, which was disheveled. There were so many things cluttering this room and that made me second-guess if I was in the right place. As I turned the corner around the couch, I noticed the rug was raised in one area at the corner. Was this a trap? Did she lift up the corner on purpose to see what I would do?' I so badly wanted to bend over and straighten out the rug but then I thought she was probably testing me. Did she want to see if I had OCD? Did she want to hear my reactions? Was this part of the therapy, part of being able to diagnose me? My guard was instantly raised.

Shortly after this obstacle, she talked about taking on things that weren't mine to take on. She had a folder in her hand and held it out. She didn't say anything but it was obvious she wanted me to grab a hold of it. So I did. Just then she shot the folder back toward herself and said, "See, you're taking on things that aren't yours to take on." That was my last visit to that therapist.

My Safe Place

But Victoria was different. Was it her smile or her tastefully decorated office? Was it the instrumental music that played in the background or the big puffy pillows that I would eventually be absorbed by? The atmosphere was exactly what I needed. Who cares if she was prettier and skinnier than I? I felt safe and that mattered. She was probably a few years older than I but on many occasions I craved motherly attention, later being diagnosed with a detachment disorder. Basically, I would see older people and want them to be my mother or father. Or I would have a physical desire to be held by them. If I felt safe, I wanted to be held.

ED was the result or byproduct of a life coming unraveled. He was the one I ran to when I felt out of control. Not that he would hand the reigns over for me to control my life, but our relationship allowed me to feel like I was in control. It was all psychological, but I knew life was unraveling when I began to restrict food. I loved the feeling of hunger. Was it the feeling of emptiness that I enjoyed? Or was it the fact that at every growl of my stomach, I knew I was in charge? Either way, ED was easy to spot, at least to me anyway. To others, they had no idea.

Victoria continued, "How long have you struggled with an eating disorder?"

"It all started when I was 14 years old. I've gone cold turkey off and on since then but I can never seem to completely severe ties with ED," I said, matter of factly.

"ED. Is that what you call your eating disorder?" she asked, with a kind smile.

"Yeah, I believe he is a force that has great power over me," I responded.

"What do you mean by power?" she continued the questioning but in a very non-judgmental tone.

"It's like I'm in a trance and he influences my decisions," I said, trying to make it make sense.

"Do you ever tell him no?" she continued.

"That's a really good question. I've never really thought about it. I guess not because he always makes me think his ideas are my own. I don't realize at the time that I'm being influenced or controlled by ED until I've acted on bulimia or restricting," I said, looking at the wall as if I was pondering my own words.

"Do you believe ED comes out at certain times? Like tell me what has been going on in your life this month?" she continued, asking me questions I hadn't thought about in years.

I replied, "I guess he comes out when I'm feeling like I have no control over my choices."

"What choices have been made for you lately?" she solemnly asked.

"I'm not really sure. I guess it's just a feeling like I don't have control. Like our church is not growing and my kids don't need me as much anymore. My sisters and I aren't on good terms. And I'm feeling overwhelmed at work," I answered, hoping she wouldn't go any deeper on day one.

I left that first session with my head spinning. I felt like I had more questions leaving than when I came in. Why did I seek counseling again? Was my goal to be cured of my eating disorder? Did I want to know why I stumbled into bulimia to begin with? Would my counselor be able to open up my memory box that had been sealed since childhood? I had a lot to process. She wanted to see me every week for the first two months and go from there. I scheduled my next appointment and left.

I felt hopeful. I liked Victoria's method. I felt comfortable, challenged, and actually excited to get the help I knew I needed. I continued my counseling with her for a year. She was certified in EMDR (eye movement desensitization and reprocessing). She introduced this therapy early on in our counseling sessions. It was highly effective. Though I didn't understand how holding onto vibrating pods could help rewire my brain, I knew it was working. I was beginning to take some old wounds and file them away as an old memory instead of a traumatic event that was ongoing. Everything from my sister's abuse to fears of my children not being protected was discussed and processed.

I felt like I didn't need ED anymore. I believed I was capable of utilizing other coping skills, like journaling or taking a walk. As long as I continued to process my emotions in real time, I felt powerful and in charge. Everything was going great until the day I walked in on Brenna.

Chapter 23

My Worst Nightmare

I tried keeping my eating disorder a secret from my family growing up and then from my children after I grew up. I thought I had done a good job at hiding my struggle. I remember witnessing Mom go on diets all the time when I was a kid. She never liked the way she looked which inadvertently made me question if I was good enough. The media answered that I was not. No one was ever good enough. I needed this fad diet or these new shakes. I needed this hairstyle or these fashion items. We were bombarded with advertisements that promised us happiness if only we'd buy their products. No wonder Mom, and then later I, were never satisfied with ourselves. We had magazines telling us this lie since we were teens.

Brenna was an active girl. From the time she took her first step, she was doing something—running, jumping, spinning, you name it. She loved gymnastics and volleyball. She enjoyed hiking and biking. She could not sit still. Even when she got to high school, she was active as a member of the band. But somehow the vicious lies that say you're not good enough eventually fell on Brenna's ears. She was taken captive and began a secret life of her own.

"What are you doing?" I screamed, as I accidentally walked in on Brenna in the bathroom.

"Nothing!" she barked back, but it was too late. I knew exactly what was going on.

Brenna had been taken captive by ED. My worst nightmare came true. The one thing I tried to shelter my children from had gone after my child. Brenna was throwing up and somehow I knew it wasn't because she was sick. I knew I had just walked in on our next battle.

That weekend I was scheduled to go away for a pastors' wives retreat. It was going to be three days of connecting with other wives, hearing women's stories, and taking a break from ministry. I was looking forward to it until that moment. I told Caleb what I just found out and told him I wasn't going to go to the retreat. I needed to be there for Brenna.

"You have to go," he strongly stated.

"No, I can't. I'm needed here," I responded with no thought to what he was saying.

"It's important you get away. I'll be here with the girls. Once you get back, we'll tackle this," he said, as calm as could be.

I was angry. Once again I had no control. I couldn't prevent Brenna from harming herself and now I couldn't stay home to be with her. I told Caleb I would go to the retreat but I wasn't going to be able to relax.

The Retreat

I don't want to be here, I kept telling myself

again and again. This was going to be the worst weekend. I knew I needed to be at home with my baby. What good would it do me to be two hours away from where I felt I was most needed? And I was not feeling like talking to anyone, not even my good friends who also went to the retreat. They knew something was up but I wasn't talking. Usually I would try and cover up the fact that I was mad or upset, but that weekend I didn't have the strength to be someone else.

The first activity we did was take a God walk. We had spent the previous hour worshiping, singing, and listening to a lady share her trial and how she overcame it. Now it was time for us to be alone with God and talk with Him about our own struggles. I wasn't exactly reverent. I was still in shock of walking in on Brenna throwing up. And my anger overwhelmed me. Instead of going to God for help and understanding, I lashed out.

"Why would You let this happen to my little girl?" I quipped. "Hasn't she been through enough with my crazy family? You knew my worst fear was for my children to battle ED and You chose not to intervene?" I had no strength to continue fighting God. I was exasperated. I finished my walk with the silent treatment.

I got back to the retreat center and took my seat. I'm sure my face showed my disgust. If that didn't give off the impression I wasn't okay, I'm certain my aura did. I kept to myself as the day continued.

"Who wants to share about their time with God?" the leader asked.

For the next hour I tried to stomach how the

Lord met with everyone and how close they felt to him. *Of course he did,* I flippantly said to myself.

The night came and went. My friends and I made small talk but I was truly not in the mood for socializing. I just wanted to go to my room and call home. "Hi, how is Brenna?" I asked, hoping the nightmare was over because I overreacted.

"She's been in her room a lot today. I think she's embarrassed and fearful because she's not sure how you're going to handle this when you get back," he said, trying to be as helpful as he could.

"I'm really scared, Caleb. I hope we caught it in time. If not, it's going to be a long road to recovery," I explained, trying to stay positive.

"Well, let's get her in to see the doctor next week and go from there," and with that, Caleb hung up.

I was surprised I got a good night's rest. I woke up less angry but still not wanting to be there. I made my way to the cafeteria and sat at a table with a few of my friends, listening to them talk about how much they were enjoying this retreat. By then, I had enough strength to present a smile. I was here whether I liked it or not, so I decided to make the most out of what was left of the weekend.

For our second activity, we took another walk around the retreat center but this time we were instructed to seek God with all our heart, mind, and soul. I found my way off the path toward a creek. The water was moving slow and rhythmic. For the first five minutes, I just stared at the water. I watched the leaves float by while I thought about home. After about ten minutes, I cried out to God.

"Lord, if You want me to trust you then You have to show up right now," I whispered. Just then a small tear rolled down my cheek. I was starting to feel emotion other than anger. I felt sadness. I felt fear. I walked back to the room where we were gathered.

"So who wants to share about their time with God?" the leader asked again.

I listened more attentively this time. I thought maybe God would show up through someone else. Maybe their story would be something I could grab onto. Or maybe a worship song would be just the promise I needed to be reminded of. And though it was nice to hear how God met these women on their walks, I wasn't sensing anything was for me. I wasn't mad. I guess I was just resolved to feeling hopeless.

Stepping Out In Faith

The next day was Sunday, the last morning of the retreat. I was anxious to get back home and hug my girls. I found my seat in the conference room and waited for the finale. What would the leaders do to end the retreat? This was the last chance for God to respond to my creek-side cry.

"This morning we are going to take some time and pray for one another," the main leader said. "I know many of you have come face to face with some struggles this weekend and we want to give you an opportunity to be prayed over. So who would like to be brave and sit in this chair and tell us what you want God to do for you?" she challenged, motioning to a single chair in the front of the room.

Many ladies, one by one, went up to share

and be prayed over. There were about four women who stood around them, ready to speak the very words God would place on their lips. There was one lady in particular who had a very sad story. As she shared it and how God met her on her different walks, she began to sob. The hurt and pain were pouring out of her while these woman caught her tears and carried her burdens to God. The deep anguish of decades of pent up pain was being released into the arms of women who sincerely loved her. It was beautiful.

I sat in my chair at the back debating whether I wanted to go up. Would I find relief? Would my story be rewarded with prayers like I had just witnessed. Would these peers of mine reject me once I shared my ugly story? Time was running out. I needed to make a decision. I had every prompt from the Holy Spirit to go up so it wasn't like I was waiting for God to speak. By not going up I would be rejecting God's hand for mercy. What was holding me back? Why was this decision so difficult for me? I was drowning in fear and there was God throwing me a life preserver.

"I want prayer more than I want isolation," I said to myself. I got up out of my seat and began to make the walk to the front of the room. I was so nervous, for stepping out in fear is always risky—but not with God. He promises to walk and stand with us—even cry with us. I needed to trust His promises despite my insecurities.

This walk was a defining moment for me. I told myself that I can be brave, that I can trust others to carry my burdens. "Come have a seat, Alora," the leader gently said, with a smile that conveyed she was proud of me. This was not just the leader of the group, she was the wife of my boss. I was also in front of the district superintendent's wife. Sitting at a table was the wife of the pastor who served at the church we were currently pastoring at. There were my good friends and some ladies I had never had a conversation with before. I sat down and instantly the weight of shame pushed my head down.

"Alora, thank you for coming up and trusting God to meet you in this space. Please share with us what God has been doing for you this weekend," she gently requested.

To tell them my pain over Brenna meant I needed to share my own struggle with an eating disorder. I began with that. As I spoke, I felt comfort, like the comfort I felt falling off the cliff. I knew I was safe. This was a sacred place. My story would be handled with care by these women who truly loved me.

I began with my own struggle with ED starting at 14 years old. I talked about my fears of being found out and then about my hospitalizations. Of course, I condensed almost 30 years in about five minutes. Then I talked about the pain I had walking in on Brenna. Instantly I began to cry. It started off with a tear running down my cheek, but then I felt the tidal wave of emotions coming once I said I felt so much guilt. That was the source of the pain. I felt extreme heavy guilt that I was the reason Brenna was now battling an eating disorder.

Just then I felt hands on me, one on my shoulder, then one on my back, one on my knee, and then one on my head. I was covered. There was no place I didn't feel covered by these godly women. Women brought me tissues and then the prayers began. God was in this place. He was receiving their prayers and replacing the pain with hope and peace. After a few minutes of prayers, the leader asked me what I was feeling.

"I feel peace," I said smiling for the first time all weekend.

"Now I want you to pray to God. I want you to tell Him what you want Him to do for you," she directed.

At this point, my nerves about going up were gone, and I was desperate. This was my time to come face to face with my Maker and tell Him exactly what I needed from Him. I knew my Savior so I knew this wasn't sitting on Santa Claus's lap and asking for a laptop. This wasn't making a birthday wish as I blew out candles. This was weighty. This was intimate. This was holy.

"God, I need You to intervene right now. I need You to run to Brenna and speak into her heart, that she is good enough, that You see her. God, I need You to take away my guilt. I feel so ashamed. Please take my pain and tell me it's going to be okay," I pleaded, as tears continued to stream down my face.

Suddenly, I was transformed. I felt whole again. I felt lighter. I had hope. It was time to go home. What had God done in Brenna's heart? What road lay ahead for us? I knew it was going to be a journey, but I was no longer afraid of it. I was eager to see God's hand move.

Chapter 24

The Nightmare Continues

I came home a different person. I had come face to face with my grief and left it at the cross. I was hopeful for what would come next. The girls weren't sure how I would handle the situation. I had always been in between a helicopter mom and an involved parent—maybe a little too involved. But they knew I loved them and that I would show up any time they needed me to. I always told myself that when I had kids, I would not only say I loved them but I would show them as well.

For the next year, Brenna saw a doctor who monitored her health. She would have bi-weekly weigh ins, talk with a nutritionist, and have an exam to make sure she was physically okay. At the same time, we had her see a counselor. I knew all about ED and how he draws you in. But I also knew that she probably was feeling like she had no control. The last thing I wanted to do was violate any safe spaces she had created. So though I was very curious how her counseling was going, I gave her space and told her she could talk with me any time about her struggle but she would have to initiate it.

Simultaneously, I continued seeing Victoria. It was ironic that both Brenna and I were seeing a counselor for an eating disorder. At the same time, I was able to work through my fears that had become a reality. Victoria knew that the eating disorder was just the coping skill I choose when trouble came. So she began the search for the real culprit, the thing that I had buried or blocked out.

I continued my treatment with EMDR. I would always close my eyes and see a bird flying in the sky. At times, I would be sitting on this bird as he flew over the land. That was my safe place, high above anything and anyone. No one could hurt me while I was up in the sky. But then I would always switch to standing in front of a brick wall. At times I was an adult trying to break through the wall. Other times my teenage self would try. I had big gaps from my childhood that I couldn't remember, Diane's abuse being one of the them. But I knew if I could just push through this wall, I would be able to uncover the truth.

With me being in counseling and Brenna being treated for her eating disorder, Shiloh fell through the cracks, though I didn't know it at the time. Shortly after we moved to Ohio, she struggled with anxiety about going to school. But after she got involved in the band, she found a home and her anxiety went away—or at least I thought it did.

Shiloh and I didn't quite see eye to eye. She was quite outspoken and opinionated. She spoke with me directly and at times very harshly. I had trouble relating to her. I knew if I could get past the porcupine quills, I would find my sweet Shiloh who would melt in my arms—but that rarely happened. In fact, the closer I got to Shiloh, the greater the risk of being hurt. That's the reason I kept my distance. She and Caleb were like two peas in a pod, not like they were best friends but they were both direct. Brenna and I had more in common because we wore our hearts on our sleeves and were driven by empathy. Caleb and Shiloh were both opinionated and at times would duel it out.

Shiloh Backstage

Shiloh was a dancer and loved everything about dancing. As a kid, she took ballet and lyrical. She loved the freedom she experienced when she danced. She was delicate and she commanded the stage with every pirouette and plie. She dreamt of being a dancer on Broadway. Because of her love of dance, she joined the school band's color guard. She handled everything from spinning a flag to twirling a wood rifle with poise. Not only did she have to learn the aerodynamics of spinning and throwing, but she had to learn the choreography of the routine. For some, this would be an impossible task, but for Shiloh, it was second nature.

As I witnessed beauty cascading all around, I didn't think I had anything to worry about with Shiloh. She was taken care of and I could put her on the back burner to simmer. Brenna was the one who was struggling and needed full attention.

It's funny how we can navigate life like cooking. Some things are front and center, while other things just sit and wait their turn. This is how I parented Shiloh and Brenna. One was in triage while the other waited in the waiting room. I had no idea that by parenting this way, I was losing my 'well' daughter to other dangers.

During this time, Caleb was pastoring a church in Millhaven, Ohio. It was a good church and the people were friendly. However, there was a lot of work to be done in motivating a group of people who were more comfortable remaining in holy huddles than searching for the lost. Even new people who browsed our church were intimidating the members. Not everyone reacted the same way but the ones who had control preferred keeping the church a tight-knit group of people who knew one another well. This resulted in a small youth group. The whole time we were there the group never really grew and our girls were eventually bored by it. They began to focus their social life on school friends and left their church life to just Sundays.

At the time, I was happy to have them going to church. I knew many kids were growing up in homes without hope. Even if our group was small, God was big. As long as they continued hearing the Word, they would know the truth. I had no idea the struggles I was going through with Brenna was just the beginning of an avalanche of pain that was to come. I would eventually come face to face with the enemy who would kidnap my girls right before my eyes and it happened out of nowhere.

What started once as a beautiful weekend turned into a nightmare that I was left to carry on my own. If it wasn't for the prayers of many friends and the promises of God, I wouldn't have made it through. I journaled about this story as the nightmare was being lived out. Here's the raw truth.

Coming back home from a wonderful weekend in Cincinnati with Shiloh on a school bus, I reached out to Brenna via text, who was at home that weekend with her dad. She had taken him to the airport earlier that morning and was excited to head over to Firestone High School to watch her high school's indoor percussion team perform. Her boyfriend and a few friends were among the most important people she was excited to see. Earlier in the week, Brenna had noticed a few of these friends icing her in the hallways at school. It was starting to become obvious to her that she was being pushed out of the friend group and so she wanted to try and mend things by going and supporting them.

After a few months of withstanding judgments and outright division from her so-called friends for dating Derek, a fellow friend in this friend group, she was left blindsided when Derek started ignoring her as well that week. Hoping for a reset, she went to the competition to show her support for her friends, but sadly realized that the friend group, once her lifeline, was done with her. The coldness she felt in the hallways at school was not paranoia, but a painful reality. The truth became unbearable to handle.

And this is where I found myself, riding the school bus almost four hours away from my daughter. In response to my text of 'how's it going?' she sent me a picture of her crying and told me she was sad. I was hoping her time at the competition would turn things around for her, but what actually happened that night changed the course of our family's life forever.

Chapter 25

The Darkest Night

I had pulled double duty over the previous few months trying to be there for both daughters, as they slowly started to descend into self-hatred, self-harm, and suicidal ideation. Brenna for three years had battled bulimia and had started cutting as a coping skill. Shiloh was extremely deficient in self-esteem and self-confidence, which led to her threatening suicide multiple times. My life had become a constant chess game of second-guessing, paranoia, and walking on egg shells. It was just as unstable and life altering with every conversation as a Jenga tower. So knowing she was home alone and my help four hours away, I entered the throne room through prayer.

God had always been my go-to when things seemed bleak and I had absolutely no control over any given situation. God would reveal to me that He didn't want to be a runner up or a last resort. It's amazing how surrender and submission are easily activated in a safe worship setting, lifting my hands up while singing Chris Tomlin's *Good, Good Father*.

But when the rumbling of thunder and the cresting of waves hit, it's Mom to the rescue. My surrender and submission take a back seat until my plan doesn't work. Was it pride? A trust issue? Could it be an automatic innate reaction to protecting my family? The irony lies in the fact that the One who loves my children more than I, the One who knows what they need and don't need, and the One who has the power to redeem any and all situations is the One I push to the back seat.

As I look back over the text messages during that bus drive, I noticed I told her not to be depressed. Really? I told her to try and enjoy her own company. This was a futile attempt to put a band-aid on a wound that needed a tourniquet. To make matters worse, my husband had left that morning for a week with the National Guard. We had made a decision earlier in the year that when he was away with the military, I would not inform him of things going on back home about which he couldn't do anything. But the weight of this unknown was heavy. Would I find her out with friends? Would she self-harm in an attempt to feel better? Would the words I texted her, exempt of the Spirit's guidance, make everything worse by making her feel like a failure if she continued to be depressed?

I occasionally sent a text asking what her plans were. She said Milly, her on-again, off-again best friend, would be taking her out for food. Finally, I could breathe. It wasn't that I believed this would end all of her problems, but that it would give her a chance to distract herself. I had texted her every hour asking her how it was going. The helplessness I felt triggered my own childhood memories of not being protected. All my futile attempts of trying to protect my children from being harmed or feeling sad had been a way to overcompensate for what I wanted my family to do for me.

But what I had inadvertently done their whole lives was insulated them from a world full of evil intent and self-preservation at all costs. Their emotional immunity wasn't built up to handle disappointment or betrayal from friends, so even the hint of conflict or outright ditching them left them inadequate to bounce back. This caused them to believe the only logical reason for friends leaving was due to them not being worthy or good enough. This became the fuel for the internal conversation that said, *If I don't matter, then what's the point of living?*

Shiloh and I got home late that night. I received a text that Brenna was also on her way home. On the trip I had wrestled with feeling a bit left out by Shiloh. It was bittersweet. On one hand I was so happy to see her engaged, laughing, and bonding with her guard team. But as I saw other moms, who had come to chaperone, sitting with their daughters during down times and Shiloh opting to sit with her friends, I couldn't help feel this was a missed opportunity to bond with my daughter or my daughter to bond with me.

We had had many discussions over the past few years of how she didn't have many friends and would prefer to stay inside and watch Netflix in her room. She didn't feel like she fit in anywhere, and this started to erode her self-esteem and self-confidence. So listening to her laughing and watching her connect with the group brought a smile to my heart. Get over it, Alora, was how I decided the trip would go. When you're a parent, sometimes your needs have to take a back seat in order to affirm your child or allow your child to flourish. That night on the bus ride home, Shiloh was completely oblivious to her emotions that would soon erupt and change the course of her life as well.

Bree got home shortly after we did. Shiloh and the team had received the highest score their school had ever received for Winter Guard and she was very excited to share her weekend with Brenna. However, Bree was still in the depression pit and having burger with a friend would not be enough to pull her up out of it. In the middle of Shiloh beginning to tell her about her trip, she got up and said she was just going to bed. The next few minutes were a bit of a blur, most likely caused from the reality that I was still in the trenches of this battle with no hope in sight.

Shiloh and I ended up in my room. I tried to tell Shiloh that we needed to understand what Bree was going through and put our needs on the shelf to take care of those we love who are hurting. This did not sit well with Shiloh because to her it was always about Brenna. I later realized I had constantly been putting her on the back shelf for the previous two years while I tried to fix Brenna. In hindsight, I think I did more damage. Fortunately, God takes all our messes and redeems them and creates beauty from ashes.

Shiloh said something flippant on her way

out of my room that I can't remember but that hit a button that caused my lid to flip. I got up from my bed and slammed my door. I sat back down on my bed and just started crying. The slamming of the door caused the girls to run into my room and ask what was wrong. I yelled for them to close my door and just leave. They immediately thought my sisters had done or said something to me because they know that they are the only ones that can cause me to flip my lid. "No, it's you guys!" I screamed. "You can never get along. Just leave," I screamed.

This became the fuel that set the tone for the next hour. Shiloh shouted to Brenna that it was her fault because it's always about her. At this point, my door had been shut and the next thing I heard was the bathroom door slamming and a hole being punched into it. I jumped up and ran out of my room and flung open the bathroom door. The sight I saw caused my heart to sink. Brenna, in a rage, grabbed the razor on the counter and sliced her arm in two places. She was gripping her bloody arm with her hand and crying, "I didn't do anything wrong. Why am I doing this to myself?" These words will forever remain in my memory. I turned the water on and told Brenna to run her arm under the water. I suddenly found myself in an emotional, physical, mental, and spiritual triage ward.

Chapter 26

God Can't Fix Everything

Grasping for answers I screamed, "You both just lost your phones." In some way I thought social media had played a big role in this and that their phones were the source of the problem. They had become dependent on friends and communicated only through text, snapchat, and other apps. I knew friends were a big reason Bree was depressed and so I thought removing her from what was a toxic environment would be a way to remove this cancer from metastasizing. Or it could've been a way for me to regain some control of this awful situation. Shiloh stormed downstairs to go outside and cool off. I needed my family to be together so I went and told Shiloh to get back inside. "No," she screamed, to which I screamed back, "Get inside now."

Shiloh and I went back into the bathroom to see how Brenna was and as I knelt beside Brenna to clean her up I said something about God being here for her. "God can't fix everything," Shiloh said in a disconnected and cold way. She was hurting so much on the inside but all that was coming out was anger and coldness. She had built up walls hoping to protect herself from anyone hurting her again but all it did was imprisoned her with her own emotions and didn't allow for anyone to come in and help her.

Bree got bandaged up and went to her room while I continued my conversation with Shiloh about God. She had been questioning His goodness for a while. As we battled in the bathroom, she confessed she had prayed to Him for so long to help her but He never answered her. "I need proof and evidence that He exists because all I see is bad things happening in the world and Him doing nothing about it," she said, as tears flowed down her cheeks.

Immediately I felt like I had to defend God. I reminded her of my car accident miracle story and how her dad was one drink away from being an alcoholic before God made the taste of alcohol awful for him. She discredited both stories, saying my memory must have failed me as to who actually rescued me and that Dad was simply searching for something better and decided Christianity was it. After telling her she couldn't take my story, my evidence of my God, and mess with it, I said in a rebuking way, "God won't be mocked," feeling like the enemy was hovering over her. I pleaded with her to give God a chance. I put God to the test and said to give Him 30 days to show up.

She said, "if you have so much faith in your God that He loves me so much that He will show up, then after 30 days if He doesn't show up, you will let me choose my own religion?" I felt cornered.

On one hand I knew I was putting God to the test, knowing scripturally it says not to. I knew if I didn't accept her bet that I was inasmuch saying I didn't have as much faith in God that I was saying I did. On the other hand, if I said yes to the bet, I was allowing my child to walk away in search of something that would leave her even more lost. I said ok, then prayed for God to show up soon.

In the middle of triage that night, I envisioned I was in an ocean and both of my girls were drowning and I could only save one of them. My heart was torn and broken. In their own way, both girls were drowning. Later, I told a friend about this vision. "You're believing a lie that you could even save one of them. Only God can save them," she said. In an instant, that pressure released and allowed me to put my eyes back on the God I base my eternal destiny.

Shiloh wasn't satisfied with ending it there. She continued by saying, "If you have so much faith in your God, then let me raise the ante. If God doesn't show up in 30 days, then I'll kill myself. Because if your God loves me so much, then He won't want me to kill myself and will show up."

Deep down I knew Shiloh was pleading for her life to the Giver of life but at the same time, I needed to be her mom. She needed me to stand up to this nonsense she was spouting. "If you say you're going to kill yourself one more time, then I'm going to take you to the hospital and they will have to admit you," I sadly but firmly stated, trying to highlight the seriousness of her threats.

At some point of the conversation, she said

she needed help. Finally, a crack was opened. Reality had set in that she was way over her head in this emotional and mental battle. I gave her many options to consider: the suicide hotline, the hospital, counseling, medicine, or her pediatrician. She said she didn't know so I suggested she sleep on it. I told both girls that they could stay home the next day and to sleep in to get some much needed rest as it was almost midnight at that point. I would have a game plan and we would get through this. Both girls were stable and in their beds so I called it a night and crawled into my bed, praying for a miracle as tears covered my pillow. The emotional and physical scars that took place over that hour only served as the beginning. I had no idea that it could get worse, but it did.

After a restless night, I got up and got ready for work. I intended to call off, but the idea of having some dear friends at the office covering me in prayer propelled me to go in. I work with some of the most godly leaders I have ever met. I find deep significance and purpose at work. I also find an abundance of hope, encouragement, and joy rubbing elbows with these spiritual giants. I'm sure they would downplay my description of them, but it's true. So without pause, I got ready and headed in.

I waited for Rosemary, our office manager, to get in an hour later and asked to meet with her. I found a safe place to share all that had happened just nine short hours earlier. With tears, she met me in my grief and crisis. Just like I anticipated, she gave me great counsel and suggested I discuss this further with our district superintendent,

Peter. I had discussed other concerns I'd had in years past with him, so I felt comfortable with that suggestion. Peter offered compassion, shared tears, and provided direction.

I've lived through crises before, which had always created more problems due to how I handled them. I was ready to tackle this one in a whole new way. I sought counsel, I prayed early, and I was open to any advice given. Struggling with control issues, I recognized early on in this crisis that I had absolutely no control over what had taken place. I knew I didn't want to revel in guilt or should haves. What was needed was a concrete, saturated-in-prayer plan about which I felt peace.

The plan was to pause. I didn't need to rush them into counseling that day, or get a prescription stat. I didn't need to call 911 or ship them off to a psychiatric ward. I needed to calmly have a discussion with my girls. They needed to know everything was going to be okay. They needed a Mom who was in control of the situation, not an out-of-control Mom freaking out, displaying a lack of trust in the God I just put to the test. More importantly, they needed grace, and a lot of it.

With Caleb gone, and a decision not to inform him of what had taken place, I felt inadequate to handle this alone. But what I had learned in recent weeks is that this was the best place for me to be for 'God to work all things out for good.' I saw Him give strength to my weak arms, a footing for my unstable feet and soundness to an unsettled mind. God ushered in all His angels He had on duty that day to sustain me. My circumstances didn't change but my posture did and that provided the hope I needed to keep walking.

Chapter 27

It's Going To Be Okay

I got home and found Brenna reclining in her favorite chair, eating breakfast and watching Netflix. It was a sight I had seen every day for the previous year. I was forever changed by the events that took place the night before, but she seemed so normal, as if the external reminder of her inner struggle didn't faze her. With almost a canned speech on my lips, all I could muster up was that I loved her so much and that it was going to be okay. I told her that I wasn't angry the night before when I slammed my door but that I was fearful.

For their entire life, I had dreamt of my girls being best friends, sharing a bond that could never be broken. I had desired that for myself my whole life, but never had it so I longed for them to have what was never an option for me. However, over their lifetime, that dream seemed to be just that—a dream that would never come to fruition. But more recently, they started becoming friends which gave me hope. So when another obstacle to their friendship arose, I lost it.

My fear of them turning out like me with my sisters was displayed as anger through the slamming of my bedroom door. I told Brenna to call her counselor and try to get an appointment sooner than her original appointment. Luckily, she was able to get one in a few days. I continued to check in with her throughout the week, almost like a mother duck with a duckling. I don't know who was more fragile. All I knew was that this wasn't over and I had to handle her with care.

That same morning, Shiloh woke up a little later. I was hoping she still wanted help and that the little crack in her walled tower was still open. Unfortunately, I was met with a harder exterior. I believe she felt vulnerable from the night before, scaring her to the point that she not only fixed the crack but laid another layer to her walls. Denial that there was even a problem was her defense. She tried to be tough, thinking this would prevent her from hurting, but all this did was imprisoned her with her demons.

She kept telling me that she would never act on her suicidal thoughts. She had said that night in triage that the only reason she didn't act on it was because she couldn't let her teammates down, but that after Guard was over, she would have nothing left to live for. She kept reassuring me that Monday morning that she was fine.

That week was pretty normal with her. She had school, practice, work, and a competition. I asked her midweek how her 30-day challenge was going. The kid that loved Awana, Sunday School, and Bible camps, and who had served in various capacities in the church and youth group, was now someone I felt I had to treat like a relative who demanded we not talk about religion or politics. My typical outspoken desire for her to see God in everything was paradoxically stifled by my desire to not push her even further away from Him.

One of the hardest things I endured that week was not being upfront with Caleb about our home life. Though we had decided together not to share, I still felt like I was being unfaithful in a sense. Later when I told him, he agreed that it was for the best.

The girls went back to school and I went back to work. That day was going to be a challenge for Brenna. She had felt the coldness from her friends the week before, which led her down a destructive path that weekend. Now she had to walk those same hallways and try to survive. I received a text an hour after she left for school that she wanted to come home because she was super sad and didn't want to be there.

I told her, "I need you to stick it out. Being alone is probably the worst things you could do. Push through it and let it all out at your counseling appointment today. Did you take your medicine yesterday?" She said she had.

My heart was breaking for her. I told her that I was praying for her and immediately went back to the well that provided for my thirsty soul. I checked back in with her at lunchtime and she said she was doing a little better. She was going to invite Derek, her boyfriend, over that night hoping her fear of him pulling away was just in her imagination. Unfortunately, she wasn't wrong.

He said he couldn't come over because his family was having a birthday party for his little brother.

    That solidified in my mind that it was over. What boyfriend doesn't invite his girlfriend over for his brother's birthday party? I knew it was only a matter of time. How would Brenna handle the break-up? Would this break her? I was happy to hear later in the week that she was sensing he was going to break up with her and she wanted to break up with him first. It seemed like she had a good perspective on the situation. But boy, was I wrong.

Chapter 28

The Secret Night

March 30, 2018

I had texted a good friend named Judith, asking if we could get together. Rosemary had suggested I talk with her about Shiloh's struggle with God since it hadn't been too long since Judith had struggled with God. We planned to meet a few hours before picking up Caleb from the airport. I needed advice on how to approach Shiloh's struggle. Of course, I had my own beefs with God over my lifetime, but I never outwardly denied Him.

In a recent conversation, Shiloh stated she did believe in God but struggled with why He allows such evil to take place. But during that awful night in the bathroom, she inasmuch cursed God. With Shiloh's outright mocking and blaspheming of God, along with me putting God to the test, I'm surprised God didn't strike us both dead. God must have showed great restraint or it could have been His overwhelming, never-ending, reckless love for Shiloh that allowed us both to take another breath.

That morning proved invaluable. The Spirit was speaking loudly and clearly through Judith, strengthening me from the heart out. I left empowered to walk this journey in complete victory. Ironically, the victory that I was reminded to walk in was achieved almost 2,000 years ago on the cross. It proved to definitely be a Good Friday.

Though I was strengthened and walking in victory, I was anxious about telling Caleb what had occurred almost a week earlier. Doing life together with your partner allows you to be in step with each other and on the same page. I had almost a week to process the events of that night I was calling Triage. Would his ability to process quickly, so as to not lose ground, take place? Would his advice line up with mine? Would he be upset that I kept this from him? These were real concerns I had but was pleasantly reassured I did the right thing and the advice given was good.

Both girls had to work that night so we didn't really get a chance to come together until the evening. Caleb hit the ground running with a Good Friday service, in the middle of a head cold he had come down with in Texas. He was so run-down but didn't show it. I believe the Lord gave him the strength to get through that weekend.

That night after work, Brenna got a text from Dan asking if he could come over so they could talk. She met him outside in the driveway and as he started with small talk, she interrupted him and asked if he was breaking up with her. He said he was because he wasn't ready to be in a relationship.

Prior to the two of them going out, he was in

a relationship with a girl for two years. Ironically, hindsight proved we were right when we said the next girl he dates would be his rebound, not that 'we told you so' was something we would've said with the fragile condition our daughter was in. She came in the house ticked off and I didn't blame her. She lost almost everything by taking a chance by dating him. Then he remained in the friend group, though fragmented, and Bree was left broken. I haven't allowed myself to wrestle with the emotions I feel towards him and the friends that betrayed her. We went to bed that night thinking she just needed to blow off steam by painting.

I laid in bed thinking and pondering how the week unfolded. I couldn't believe it had only been five days since the awful night in triage. It seemed like an eternity. Caleb instantly feel asleep, snoring louder than a freight train. I definitely wasn't able to fall asleep now.

Just then I heard Brenna go into the bathroom. I listened as the sound of water turned from a bath to a shower to a bath again. I thought that was weird. I just made a mental note of it and tried to fall asleep. Then I heard the cabinets open. Why would she be looking for medicine? It didn't make sense. I tried to listen in between snores, getting anxious to the point where I felt an unsettling in my soul. I got up and knocked on the bathroom door.

I asked her what was going on and she said she was just going to the bathroom. "Don't do anything stupid," I told her.

As her mother, I knew something wasn't right. For the previous three years, I had lived with paranoia about her throwing up and more recently about her self-harming. I just couldn't shake this eerie feeling. But I chalked it up as just paranoia and fell asleep. I would soon discover I should have listened to my inner groans and unsettled core.

We had enjoyed a wonderful Good Friday service the night before and woke up to get ready for our Easter egg hunt. Encouraged by the great turnout, we left for home to hopefully get a chance to connect with our girls. The weekend was pretty much a blur as far as any interactions with us and the girls. Between work and homework, I don't think we saw much of the girls.

Brenna ironically reconnected with Milly just the week prior, as her sister, Josie, one of the friends in her friend group, pushed her out. It was ironic because Josie was the one who she became great friends with during the ending of her friendship with Milly. Had her friendship with Milly not resurrected, the next week could've been worse.

Shiloh seemed to be doing okay. The girls were getting along and we thought the dust had settled. We had a very busy day planned the next day for Easter. We went to bed that night having no clue of the weight that had been placed on Shiloh's shoulders.

April 1, 2018

Easter morning is one of our favorite days. As Christians, this is the pinnacle celebration of what brings us hope. Without Christ's victory over death on the cross, we would remain forever dead in our sins. Our daily struggles would never kiss the promise of 'all things being made new.'

Even in the darkest night or the deepest hole, light bursts forth and breathes life back into a lifeless situation. That is what Easter is all about—bringing life from death.

As we all made our journey to church in separate vehicles, nothing seemed out of order. It was a joyous Sonrise service followed by breakfast. Sunday School then church made for one long day before it was even noon. Besides the longevity of the service, it was like any other Sunday.

However, one thing did stand out. While Caleb was preaching, Brenna kept responding to messages on her phone. Typically she was pretty respectful about not texting in church and paying attention. That morning was different. Leaning over, I gave her a disapproving mom look. She immediately put her phone down only to pick it back up a minute later after receiving another message. By the third time, I leaned over and told her if she didn't put it away, she would lose it.

There is an upside to owning and paying for things for the girls. It can be used as leverage. She told me to read her messages because they were on Snapchat, which deletes messages after a minute or so. Wanting to listen to the message, I took a picture of the message and told her I'd read it later. It was from Josie. After numerous attempts and apologizing and trying to make things right, she still wasn't sure if she could be friends with Brenna any longer.

Apparently, she was still upset that Derek and Bree were dating. Change is inevitable. And with change comes a shift in dynamics. The friend group was upset because everyone in it wanted

Derek for themselves. If they couldn't date Derek, then the second best thing was to be flirty friends. Once they started dating, that changed the group dynamics and everyone was upset. Brenna got to the point where she realized there was nothing she could do to make things work so she said she was pulling out all hope for reconciliation. She was done and once she stated that, Josie wanted more time. Talk about playing with someone's emotions.

Chapter 29

A Waged War

After church, I took a nap. When I awoke, I started cooking an Easter dinner. I made chicken, salad, and potatoes because we are non-traditionalists in how we celebrate holidays with food. I had the girls clear the table and was excited to finally enjoy a sit-down dinner together. It had been a long time since all our schedules allowed for us to be home at the same time.

Sitting at the table enjoying a home-cooked meal, I started the normal table conversation. Out of the blue, Shiloh said Brenna had something she needed to tell us, to which Brenna said, "No I don't." My first thought was she was interested in another boy. Usually when the girls playfully downplay wanting to share something, it's about a boy. I was not prepared for what came out of their mouth.

Shiloh finally got Brenna to confess. "I took a handful of my antidepressants two nights ago, the night Derek broke up with me," Brenna quickly added, "But I threw them up right after."

Just like that, our current reality was that

our two dearly-loved beautiful daughters, having so much going for them, thought ending their lives was the best option. Ironically, while we were celebrating victory over death, a slow death was taking place in my daughters' minds and souls. A war was raging that night and we were banking on our redeeming, loving Abba Father to rescue our daughters out of the pit of darkness.

Shiloh had no idea that by making Brenna confess what she had done two nights prior would grant her a one-way ticket to the hospital as well. As I made the connection of that eerie night of restlessness to the time Brenna was trying to take her life, I was stunned. Had my child been successful in her attempt to end it all that night while I was next door struggling with a feeling that something wasn't right, I would have died with her. My God not only saved her that night but He saved me as well.

Caleb, exhausted from hitting the ground running after working nonstop in Texas for a week with the National Guard, battling a cold, and being informed just two days prior of the events that took place the week before, was now being told his eldest tried to commit suicide the night he arrived home. Since Shiloh had been battling suicide ideation for the past six months and then Bree attempted, Caleb said, "You're both going to the hospital." Looking at me he whispered, "How did we get here?"

This was the right thing to do, but I will tell you I wasn't prepared for it in my own strength. Supernaturally God picked up our family and held us tight in His arms, as the waves hit and the hours turned into days. We took the phones away from the girls and told them to pack a bag. I later learned they didn't pack a bag because they thought they'd be back in their bed that night.

Driving to the hospital, you could hear a pin drop but the internal screams and cries could have been heard from miles away. We decided to go to the nearest hospital, which was Barberton Hospital. I had remained strong on the outside driving us to the hospital and walking in. Caleb was distant and quiet. As soon as we walked in, he went and sat in a corner by himself. The girls sat next to each other in another section as I checked them in. As soon as the receptionist asked me what was wrong, my punctured heart tearfully expressed that my oldest attempted suicide on Friday and my youngest had threatened suicide multiple times.

The question Caleb asked the girls was now haunting me: 'How did we get here?' Was there any chance we would return to happier times? God answered that question weeks later when He gently whispered, "You will never find joy when you are content with just being happy." Getting along, doing the right things, and being happy had become my desire for the Stone family. God's desire was for all of us to desire Him in a way we never had before. In the middle of our darkest night, that desire for God budded.

While the girls were waiting to be called back, they were whispering to each other and giggling. They weren't taking this seriously but they soon found out how serious this was. I had brought Brenna's medicine bottle with me to show the doctor. She had said she took about 20 pills but her pill bottle still had quite a bit of pills still in there. Looking at the date, the prescription should've been long gone. Putting two to two together, I realized she hadn't been taking her medicine.

I reminded her all the time or would ask her if she took it and she would always say she forgot. But she wasn't being truthful. She said she thought the medicine was just for her bulimia and since she wasn't throwing up any longer, she didn't think she needed it. At this point, I saw Caleb get up and walk away.

Then the time came for us to go back. For some reason, I thought we'd all be in the same room. So when they put the girls in their separate rooms, it dawned on me that our family would actually be divided. Caleb went with Brenna and I went with Shiloh. They had to strip down, not even wearing undergarments. Then with a hospital gown on and jewelry removed, the police came in and ran a wand up and down them to make sure they didn't have anything on them that they could use to hurt themselves or others.

I think that was when the severity of the situation hit the girls. Caleb and I texted over the next few hours asking how the other was and how the other child was. It was so difficult but needed, a wake-up call to the slow death they were living.

Two hours after we arrived, I asked Shiloh if anything had changed by being there. "I now have hope," she replied. She said she was willing to do whatever the doctor suggested. She continued, "I was afraid to get help because then I would have to admit I had a problem." The walls collapsed.

The energy and strength she was exerting to hold her walls up had to be exhausting. Allowing her walls to fall brought hope. Darkness has to flee when light shines through. The days ahead proved to be difficult but walking in them with hope kept us all going.

Chapter 30

The Hospital Stay

The decision was made that the girls would be transported to different hospitals and most likely admitted. Brenna had just turned 18 a few months earlier, so she needed to go to St. Thomas. Barberton Hospital didn't have a behavioral health ward, so they weren't able to treat them. They were only able to provide medical assessment, so they put the transfer order in.

Shiloh, only being 16, was being transferred to Millhaven Children's Hospital. Both girls would have to be transported via ambulance. At this point, they were under the care of the hospital and it was policy that if they had to transport patients to another facility, it had to be via ambulance.

While we waited for their discharge to come through, Caleb and I switched for a little while at one point so we could check on the other child. Seeing how this decision broke Shiloh and revealed hope got me praying for a similar response from Bree. Unfortunately, she wasn't there. She thought the whole ordeal was unnecessary and over dramatic. She tried saying she was

18 and couldn't be forced to go. What she didn't know is that if you attempt suicide and are taken to the hospital, the hospital then becomes the legal caretaker of that patient for up to 72 hours. Once Brenna heard that number, that became her new target for release.

We were given troubling news that there were certain visiting hours at each of the hospitals. For Brenna, it was only between 5:30-6:30 p.m. She would be transported to a foreign place, without her family, and not able to see us until the next evening. This was one of the hardest emotional hurdles for Caleb and me. We knew this was best, but we wanted to walk this journey with her every step of the way.

We drove to Millhaven Children's and found our way to where they had just dropped off Shiloh. The game plan was that we had to wait for an on-call doctor to assess Shiloh and then discuss with us the reasons that brought her in. Based on his findings, he would contact the hospital psychiatrist and give his recommendations, who would then decide if Shiloh should be admitted. Because she only had suicide ideation and not an actual attempt, an assessment needed to be completed.

The room we were in while we waited was quite sterile. Everything was bolted down and encased, even the TV. I was definitely relieved the hospitals had a protocol they followed for times like this. I later learned that Ohio is the leading state with the most suicides each year. At this point in our journey, it was around 2:00 a.m. Shiloh had fallen asleep and so Caleb and I tried to get a little shut eye while we waited for the determination.

After hours, it was determined she would be admitted. Once they made that determination, they walked us to the eighth floor where the behavioral health suicide ward was. It was 5:00 a.m. at this point. We were mentally, emotionally, and physically exhausted. Once we got up to the ward, they took Shiloh in one direction and Caleb and me into this small little room. There we were interviewed about Shiloh's symptoms, habits, family history, etc. The lady was kind and reassured us that Shiloh would be fine there.

At one point during this hour-long intake, they brought Shiloh in to say goodbye. I will never forget seeing my daughter in blue scrubs, tears running down her cheeks, scared of the unknown. We hugged her tight and told her we'd be back later that day for the visit. The visitation hours at Children's was from 5-7 p.m., which was the bookends of Brenna's visitation hours (5:30-6:30 p.m.).

Our lives would be forced to no longer live with sweeping things under the rug, settling for vague responses with underlining meanings and unhealthy coping skills. This was our one chance to get the professional help our girls needed. I was willing to do whatever the doctors and counselors suggested. My ability, or better yet inability, to control this breakdown was refreshingly replaced with a new-found trust in professionals.

The verse in Exodus 14:14 had flowed from my lips in recent months but that day this verse became my anthem: 'I will fight for you, you need only to be still.' At 6:00 a.m., we were done and escorted out of the locked unit. Leaving our daughters in the hospital was one of the hardest things we've had to do as parents, but we knew their chances of survival hinged on our follow through and complete trust in the process. Exhausted, we made our way back home just in time for me to throw some clean clothes on and make-up and head in to work.

I had every right to climb into bed and sleep the morning away, but once again I found myself needing the support and prayer of my dear staff. Even though my body begged me to shut it down, my mind was not about to turn off. Work is my go to if I want to be distracted. If I'm at home, it's cleaning. Looking back now, I definitely wanted the prayers and support but I also wanted a known factor. Everything with the girls was up in the air and with my control issues, work granted me a place to have some control over my situation.

I had informed Rosemary of the night's events while I was in the hospital along with other wonderful ladies who I go to in times of great need. Prayer was definitely lifted up that night and morning. That's the great thing about God; He never sleeps and is always working. As I've been learning more about prayer, I've realized that our prayers usually are for the pain to go away, for the nightmare to be over. But I'm learning to pray for strength to get through the storm, recognizing this is just one piece in a beautiful masterpiece God is creating.

Good Friday is only good because Sunday came. Sometimes in life we find ourselves stuck in Friday not remembering that Sunday is coming. The victory was won on Friday but no one knew it until Sunday. We only live in victory when we see the light break through, but God was teaching me that we can still live in victory during the storm. And that is what we forced ourselves to do. We lived in victory every day we went to visit our girls, even when they didn't seem to be getting better. Eventually our circumstances caught up to our hope!

Chapter 31

The Author Inside

Shortly before the girls went into the hospital, I had begun a new chapter in my life as a writer, which I had always enjoyed. As a teenager, I would write poems to express my feelings. Most often the writings were dark and hopeless in nature. Over time, my dark poems turned into songs of hope. I found a deep connection with God through the lyrics. I even sang one of my penned songs at my grandfather's funeral and recorded one I wrote specifically for my father entitled 'Modern Day Job.'

As I learned more about myself through therapy, I wrestled with finding purpose in my life. I knew God created every person with a purpose and it was our duty to discover that purpose. However, I realized that I would never discover it if I still struggled with an identity crisis. Through reflecting on what God says about identity, I penned my first article called 'The Search for Identity.' I found enjoyment writing and that day began the first of many writings.

After the incident with the girls, I felt

compelled to write about Shiloh's rebellion against God. I felt like I had tried to defend God months prior in the triage room. But God showed me that He's a big God who doesn't need defended. But He does ask us to proclaim Him. With that I wrote 'Defending God and Proclaiming God are Worlds Apart.'

Defending God and Proclaiming God are Worlds Apart.

I found myself one spring defending my God to someone who was spewing offenses about His power, existence, and goodness. Fearful that God would strike this person down right in front of me for speaking so carelessly of Him, I found myself trying to force feed her a truth sandwich. It broke my heart to hear such error and nothing I said made her pause to consider I could be right. In fact, it made her dig her heels in even more and left me spiritually drained.

I left that encounter believing I had done God a favor. I clung to the promise that His word would not return void. Over the next few days, I didn't see any movement toward God's side. What I did notice was a harder shell starting to form. I met with God daily, trying to will the Spirit's affirmation that all would be okay and that the words I spoke would eventually sink in. Every chance I had to speak truth to this person, I would take it. I believed if I continued pounding her with the knowledge of His word and the reminder of the Way, she would soon believe, repent, and be spared of the lightning bolt that I feared was one slur away from detonating. Again, I found myself spiritually drained.

In times of overwhelming fear, we long to control things—or at least I do. With sincerely good intentions, we can try to do the Spirit's work in our own weak power. And then we wonder why we find ourselves spiritually drained. Defending God out of our flesh does nothing to illuminate truth. But when we allow God to meet us in the power of His Spirit, our eyes are opened, paving the way for God to be proclaimed, not defended.

I realized the truth sandwich I was trying to force feed was my own futile attempt at believing my own truth about God. God showed me that He doesn't need me to defend Him but wants me to trust Him. He didn't need me to do Him any favors, but to get out of His way.

A few months later I was granted another opportunity to speak truth to this person. In love and not fear, I found myself proclaiming God. The choices were still the same and still hers to make but fear did not win that night—the Spirit did. And it was then that I saw the hardened shell start to soften.

I found such healing with every word and sentence. I was able to share an article with our denominational district while I worked there. Many people reached out and shared their similar concerns. They too had found themselves trying to defend God with friends and family. This article gave them another perspective. I thought maybe my purpose was to help others through writing.

The girls continued to do the work of getting better after their stay in the hospital by going to counseling, taking medication, and utilizing healthy coping skills. And though they were doing better, I needed to know what had caused them to want to end it all. Did something happen to them that I had missed? Was there a secret they were keeping that would unlock the mystery? Was this just a phase or did it run deeper?

I felt like I was the best person to help my girls with their depression. I had been raised in it. Both my dad and sister suffered from depression and I wrestled with it off an on for decades. Because of my experience with eating disorders and anxiety, who better to help, right? I wish I was right but unfortunately I wasn't. I ended up putting more pressure on the girls to be transparent with me. This just created another layer of pressure that they were not prepared to carry.

For the next two years, the girls seemed to be getting better. Brenna was in weekly therapy and on medication. Shiloh was seeing a therapist as well, but her biggest hurdle was insecurity and low esteem. In the end they were being treated for not feeling good enough. I hated that the cycle repeated itself. For so many years, I couldn't say I liked myself—much less loved myself. I struggled with self-hatred and not measuring up. And then, I had a front row seat to watch my children struggle with similar weaknesses.

We celebrated birthdays and graduations. Brenna went to college and Shiloh went to work. They seemed to be getting better and enjoyed their independence, and ended up moving in together. Our girls, who I thought would never be close, were beginning to create an adult life with each of them being the other's biggest champion. We ended up leaving the church in Millhaven, Ohio and moving to Pennsylvania. I had no idea how this decision to move would affect them. Even though we invited them to come with us and even though they declined, in a sense they felt abandoned. We wouldn't know this until years later.

Chapter 32

The Breakdown

"If you spent more time with our girls than you do helping people at the church then maybe this wouldn't have happened," I barked at Caleb one night.

"Where is this coming from? I think you might be projecting onto me," Caleb calmly replied.

This night began the start of my mental breakdown. I would soon realize the truth behind Caleb's words. I had some unresolved childhood resentment that was beginning to surface. However, I thought I was justified in blaming Caleb and his attention to the church for our family problems.

"I think you might be projecting your feelings about your dad abandoning you for the church onto me," he said, hoping this would get me looking inward.

At the time we were still seeing our therapist for help with processing a huge argument we had with the girls that summer to pursue possible reconciliation. But then we transitioned to my having personal therapy for my childhood traumas. During my sessions, I would spend half the time crying and had no idea where it was coming from. All I knew is that I needed to press on, continuing to dig deep. And eventually, I would pierce the core of my issue.

It started off with jealousy. I wanted my husband to recognize me for the hard work I was doing at the church. He met with many people, training, discipling, counseling, or encouraging them. And he would come home and tell me all about the growth and healing in these people. He was making a difference in their lives. I began to feel abandoned. I wanted what he was pouring into others. It was my childhood all over again. The church became a higher priority than I and I was beginning to resent Caleb for it.

I was highly involved in the ministry of the church. I was making a difference in many people's lives through my prayer study and one-on-one discipling. But that didn't matter because I was looking for validation from one person. I thought it was Caleb so I fought for it. Eventually I would discover I was trying to get validation from my father who had long passed away. Nothing I did was going to get the praise from my dad and that became the driving force behind my breakdown.

"You have another meeting at the church?" I whined.

"It's going to be a short one. I'll be home before you know it," Caleb replied.

There was something different about Caleb. He used to be direct and confident. But the Caleb I was seeing was beginning to wear down.

I sensed he was walking on egg shells whenever I approached him. His responses were gentle but guarded. This only made me paranoid. *Why are you acting this way?* I would think. I mirrored his moves. If he seemed guarded, I put up my wall. If he seemed distant, I'd walk away. It was unhealthy behavior but in my mind I was the normal one. Caleb was the one who was acting suspiciously.

What started off as a little paranoia about Caleb blew up into a full on attack on him. He was guilty of something but I couldn't identify it. So I would continue blaming him for everything. We would have fights every day about how he's putting everyone else but me first. In an attempt to draw him closer, my actions pushed him further away. My paranoia began to spread. *Why is she asking Caleb these questions?* I would ponder. This is a basic question that you should know the answer to. *You're just trying to spend more time with my husband. I can't trust you.* Then I had two people I was watching. Would there be others?

Every interaction Caleb would have with this one particular woman made me feel betrayed. Even if I knew Caleb was going to meet with her, I felt like he was going behind my back. We talked about it and started to draw some boundary lines. "Okay, so how long is this meeting going to last with her? "

I would ask. "About an hour?" Caleb would reply.

In my mind, the boundary line that was created was one hour. If he came home later, I would become angry. Paranoia had grown into believing lies. In my attempt to create health in our relationship by drawing lines, I wore Caleb down. He no longer was happy at home. Ironically, my desire for my husband to be at home more often backfired. He no longer felt safe at home. He was walking on egg shells with me and there was no safe place to go at home. So he began to spend more time at church where he felt safe and built up.

My therapist was definitely earning her money working with me. I was so sure I was right. She didn't take sides and would press in. "Why do you think Caleb is betraying you?" she asked.

"Because he's taking time away from me and giving everybody else his attention," I replied.

"Let's talk about your father. You said he was a pastor as well?" she pivoted.

"Yes, for a short time. But he passed away in '06," I replied, irritated that we were talking about something that wasn't pertinent.

'"So tell me a little about the family dynamics when your dad was pastoring," she continued.

"Well, he would spend half his day in his office and the rest of the time helping the people in the church. My mother worked full time so she didn't feel the effects of the empty house. I would come home from school and he would be in his office with the door shut. Or he would leave to go visit people in the hospital or in their homes. I felt abandoned by my parents but thought this was normal. I didn't have many friends so I had no way of comparing family dynamics."

"When you talk about it now, what emotions are coming up?" she asked right on point.

"I feel anger. This emotion has recently taken center stage. I had never felt anger before," I said puzzled.

"The anger that you feel is being manifested as fear. And the fear is being lived out through paranoia and believing those lies," she concluded.

"So how do I address the anger?" I asked.

"You have to go back to your relationship with your father. You need to uncover your true emotions towards your dad. Start off slow. Ask yourself, 'Why am I upset that my father is doing his job?' You can ask yourself, 'How does it make me feel when he is home but not available?' Begin to sit with your emotions and work through each one until you hit unforgiveness. I'm certain you will find that once you get here, you will be ready to forgive your father," she instructed.

She continued, "You're a writer. Put into words your emotions and your feelings when you think about your dad."

This was going to be a hard request. With my jealousy turned paranoia, I saw Caleb as the current threat, not my dad. But she was the doctor. She must know something I didn't. I turned my attention and anger away from Caleb and started the road back home—back to my childhood. This relieved some pressure at home. Caleb began to relax a little, trying to encourage me to do the hard work.

I had no idea I help resentment and bitterness toward my dad. The alleged assaults were 30 years old. How could these emotions be kept alive when my father was not? I would ask myself. My therapist told me they had been buried, dormant and waiting for a time to be activated. I needed to take my feelings toward Caleb and compare them to my feelings toward my dad. It was a carbon copy. I knew then my perceived truth were lies. I began to write.

Chapter 33

The Letter

Dear Dad,

Where to start? I don't know what to say. I figured if I started writing my fingers would just continue when my mind stopped. But here I am stopped dead in my tracks. Blocked. Trying to grasp at the wind to explain why I react the way I do. My thoughts create stories void of memories. My mind continues narrating a story that hasn't even begun. So here I am looking for answers in a letter to a father who has been dead for 15 years.

I wish I could live my life void of the past. If I could wake up and just live in the moment without the fuzzy shadows of the past intruding, without my body's instinct to insulate myself every time there's a chance of being hurt. My mind seems to want to live in a futuristic fictional novel.

I know you weren't around a lot growing up. Mom can attest to that. I know you chased dreams and took us with you. I know you were never satisfied. You loved to help people but I guess we were not fixable so you went looking for other people to help. I know you loved Jesus and country. I know you loved your family but were incapable of showing it. Maybe it was easier for you to be somewhere else even when you were at home.

1. My reality has been shaped by photographs, other people's recollections, and fragmented mental clips. The dichotomy of my life is when I look through photo albums, I see smiles and laughter. I see family get togethers, presents, and outings. I see Mom and Dad—in the pictures. But then when I play the video clips in my mind, I see fear. Here are a few examples:

    a. Being chased by Diane and running to a neighboring apartment for safety.

    b. A reoccurring nightmare of being chased.

    c. A snake in our kitchen.

    d. Choking on a lifesaver and mom carrying me to a neighboring apartment.

    e. A classmate (Margaret) stealing my completed homework assignment, erasing my name and putting her name on it, and handing it in. The teacher wanted us to work it out. She ended up getting credit for it.

    f. Mom storming down to my school and giving my fourth grade teacher the riot act for allowing his students, her daughter, to kiss him before leaving for the day.

g. Spending the night at a friend's house and having her brother come home late and get beat for it. I called Mom to come pick me up.

h. That same friend yelling at me that CPS took her brother away because my mom called them.

i. Watching an RV go up in flames and hearing later that the couple was still in it.

j. I remember falling off a slide and getting the wind knocked out of me.

k. I remember getting my finger slammed in the car door and being rushed to the hospital.

l. I remember passing out in the bathroom and waking up to my mother giving me CPR.

But I don't remember much of you. I'm told you took us to the beach to find seashells and would pick up donuts for the family every Saturday morning. In a photograph, I am sitting in your log truck but I don't remember it. I am also told of your life prior to kids and how you looked at other women. I hear the sadness in Mom's voice as she tells me you didn't cheat.

I do have a memory of you screaming at the TV when the 49ers would lose and the day you told us you quit smoking. I do remember driving to Florida with my friend Heidi and the hotel messing up our reservation and having to find a place at night, hungry and tired.

I was triggered earlier this month and I linked it to you abandoning me. You never hit me or yelled at me. But how could you if you weren't ever there? I don't remember you leaving for nine months to go to Colorado Springs for school and I don't remember you being sick with cancer. Why? Why are these memories blocked? Mom tells me she was the one who handled the discipline (with Lauren and Diane). Apparently, I was a perfect child. So did you guys just put me on simmer while you dealt with an out-of-control Diane and a mouthy Lauren? Was my crime that I was perfect?

I don't know if you ever look down and see me. I don't know if you even have memory of being a father since the afterlife is a little vague in the Bible. They say there will be no more tears in heaven so I guess you're not looking down. Because I would imagine you would weep. How would one not be broken to watch his bride count the days you left her; month after month and year after year? How do your eyes not well up seeing your family be torn apart and left on mute?

I have these things against you that I am wrestling over:

1. Abandoning me emotionally.
2. Not showing interest in my life (when I got married and had kids you began to).
3. Preaching a message that at times I don't think you agreed with or at least lived out.

4. Spewing negativity and disappointment.

5. Stepping out and having emotional attachments with others.

6. Being proud of my accomplishments but not ever sitting down and having a conversation with me about them.

7. Shutting down any conflict preferring to stop the noise and sweep hurts under the rug.

8. Not encouraging my walk with the Lord but rather modeling legalism.

So where do I go from here? If I read this to you while you were still alive, would you seek forgiveness? Would you own your part in my dysfunction? Would you have regrets? Would you be interested in my life? Would you stand up for me?

Of course, this one-sided conversation is left unanswered. Do I hold unforgiveness in my heart towards you? I don't think so. But just in case, "Dad, I forgive you. I forgive you for all of the above." And I commit myself to the Father to be filled again with the ability to forgive. Only through God can I offer forgiveness. I don't hold my childhood against you. It is time to move on. It has taken too much space in my present and is jeopardizing my future. So Dad, I love you. I accept your failure as a father.

But I will accept it at face value. I won't justify it just because you were abandoned by your father as well. I won't gloss over it because of your time in Vietnam. I won't allow myself to be minimized because you tried. No—you failed as a father. You did not protect me. You did not love me the way I needed to be loved. You were not faithful to your family. You criticized, judged, and ridiculed others in the presence of God and family. You modeled hypocrisy and anger. You sat idle and did not stop the abuse that Diane was heaping on me. You went chasing your dreams, buying things you couldn't afford, while mom worked two jobs and searched sofa cushions for money for bread. You abandoned us and left us to fend for ourselves. That is your charge and one that I am offering forgiveness for.

The curse stops now. I will no longer pay for your sins. I will no longer borrow my future to pay for the past you left me with. I am taking back my life! I have a voice. I have control. I have power. I have choices. I have victory.

I can now say it wasn't the best childhood. But I have a great life now!

To all the praise and glory to my mighty King and almighty God!

Chapter 34

Deconstructing Me

The letter proved to break down some pretty sturdy walls. I was able to start putting things into the right perspective. I realized I had put unrealistic expectations on Caleb to fix my insecurities, abandonment issues, and unworthiness. The Lord was working on my heart and in my soul.

All or nothing has been my default for 47 years. But then I realized there is a third option. And this option typically lies in between. I started a deconstruction process around this time which was the most painful blessing with which God had gifted me. What do I mean by deconstructing myself? I'm giving the Holy Spirit full access to search me and highlight any areas of my life that don't reflect Jesus. And whatever doesn't has to go. This is the painful part because God will either burn it off in the refiner's fire or cut it out. Both require surrender and dependence.

- It's humbling to see yourself through the Holy Spirit's eyes rather than your own. We have no idea how much we operate in the flesh until we measure it up against the Spirit. I believed that after I was done deconstructing myself, I would be ready for God to reassemble me back to His original hope for me. I hoped it would be a warrior princess for the King!

As I wrestled with this process, I identified some areas that needed to go:

1. Being negative
2. Not trusting
3. Living and making decisions in fear
4. Not loving people where they're at but rather where I want them at.

Jeremiah 18:1-6 became my biblical source for my deconstruction plan with God. Verse four summed it all up: 'But the jar he was making did not turn out as he had hoped, so he crushed it into a lump of clay and started over." I was the lump of clay and I was being crushed for the sole purpose of being rebuilt. I started my building project with this prayer:

Dear Lord,

Can I still call You Lord even if I wrestle with trusting You? And can I still call on You when half the time I don't obey You? Following You seems like it should be so simple: listen, hear, obey, repeat. But half the time I don't even choose to listen for You as I go about my day. How can I obey You if I don't hear You and how can I hear You if I don't listen? This is my problem. But the root of the problem is the answer to the question of why I don't listen for You. I've been in this place many times to know it doesn't end well for me. So why do I continue to live in rebellion against You? How long will I choose to live each day not addressing the obstacles that have come between You and me? This only leaves me vulnerable to enemy abduction or worldly absorption.

So what are the obstacles are that are intruding in our relationship? I believe they are resentment and disappointment which has led to walled-off life void of trust. Resentment for allowing so many things to go awry or worse yet choosing these things to happen to me just to test me. To build up my strength in You—my endurance to run the race and win. I am sadly disappointed that my whole life of wholeheartedly chasing after You has brought me to this place. It's like You brought me to the top of the mountain and when the enemy had his way with me, Your hand was not there to keep me from falling. And I have fallen hard. The fall left me numb for a while. And now I'm waking up and feeling completely vulnerable to the debris that continues to fall. Because when I fell, the terrain fell with me almost burying me like an avalanche.

The only thing I have to offer is my desire to get close to You again. I am willing to listen, to hear, to obey, to repeat. But You must help me address these erosive barriers. I am pleading with You to stop the avalanche. Protect Your child. Take me by the hand and lead me out. Transform my heart from resentment to peace; from disappointment to anticipation. Increase my faith that I might be brave enough to take the next step. Don't hide Your face from my eyes. Don't remove Your angels from my side. Take my hand and whisper Your sweet love words into my heart that I might not turn my glance from You. You are great. You are holy. You are worthy. I am human. I am imperfect. I am so unworthy. But what I have to offer You, I give without delay from this day forward.

In faith,
Alora

Phase 1

The first thing that needed to go was being negative. This was difficult since I grew up in a negative atmosphere. I believed the glass was always half empty. I always saw the negative before the positive. Even if it was sun shining out, it was too breezy. Even if I went out to eat, I'd complain the food wasn't worth the money. My entire outlook was to see the black spot on the white wall no matter how little the spot was compared to the size of the wall.

Caleb was the opposite of me. If it rained, he'd wait to see the rainbow. If we went out to eat, he'd have fun because we were together even if the food was terrible. And if a spot was on the wall, he'd hang a picture over it! He was always looking for the positive in every situation. He would usually be the high tide that made my ship rise, but no longer was this the case. His resiliency was really low and he began to feel the effects of low-grade depression.

I started to implement intentional positivity into my daily routine. I made a point to see the good with every obstacle, every annoyance. Like any habit, after a few weeks this was getting easier to do. Before I knew it, I didn't have to be intentional. Positivity started flowing out of me.

Phase 2

Not trusting was the next big construct that needed to collapse. I was skeptical of everyone—their actions, motivations, and responses. I had a narrative that I would play in my mind. If I sent a text to someone and they didn't reply fast enough, I began to create a storyboard that they were mad at me and thus were no longer a safe person. I began to itemize what they knew about me. What secrets did I tell them? How could I pull out of the friendship first to save a little rejection? More often than not, they would always reply starting with 'sorry for the delayed response' or 'sorry I didn't have my phone with me.' Hours of worry and strategy were unnecessary. It left me so brittle.

Caleb was my person. I trusted him with my life. I trusted him with my heart. He had never caused me not to trust him. I knew everything about him and he knew everything about me. He was safe. He held my secrets and dreams. He knew my insecurities and struggles. He knew just what to say and what to do to make me feel loved. But during this time, I no longer trusted him. In my breakdown, I felt he was choosing others over me. I felt he cared more for the church than he did for me and our marriage. He became unsafe. I felt I couldn't share my concerns with him without feeling attacked. I believed he invalidated me all the time. He was guilty and continued doing things he knew I didn't approve of. I felt disrespected and abandoned. The only thing he would say in response was, "You're believing lies. I do love you. I do care about you. I'm not choosing the church over you." But to my inability to trust anyone, I felt I was being played.

It would take the work of the Holy Spirit to recalibrate my trust meter. It would also take establishing realistic boundaries and keeping to them. If Caleb said he had a meeting, he would give me an estimated time it would take and stick to it. If it was going to go over, he would text me. I had lost the ability to depend on Caleb. But this was just because my expectations were sky high. In my inability to feel complete, I wanted to control him. So I had to remember that God would be the only one who could rebuild me to wholeness. I began to slowly let go of a lot of my expectations.

Phase 3

The third deconstructive phase was to let go of fear. I had been swallowed up by fear. I made decisions through the grid of fear. I lived life paralyzed by fear. Fear was debilitating me. Is Caleb going to leave me? Am I going to be alone for the rest of my life? Those questions would play in my head. I couldn't seem to go a day without fearing for my life in some way or another. I was still believing the enemy's lies, so everything I thought about was deemed as a real threat. I didn't understand why Caleb wasn't as concerned as I was.

God gives us 365 verses in the Bible to conquer fear, one for every day of the year. "Fear not for I am with you." It's so simple, yet so hard to do. The first thing I needed to do was listen to God more than I listened to Satan. I had to relearn God's voice because I had many voices vying for my attention. If I was going to be able to detect the lies, then I needed to first know the truth. So if the enemy said that God doesn't love me any longer, I could combat that threat with John 3:16: "For God so loved the world ..." If I didn't submerge myself with the truth, the lies would take me under. With my propensity towards negativity, it was easier to believe the lies than the truth. I had to work twice as hard relearning the elementary truths about God and His word.

Phase 4

This last phase in the building project was loving well. I struggled with loving people where they were instead of where I wanted them to be. This was most evident in my relationship with Shiloh. My good friend, Brittany, called me one day and said she had heard from the Lord. It was a message but she was worried about sharing with me because it was heavy. However, she was trusting she heard clearly from the Lord and He was telling her to share it with me. She called me and began to share these tender words from the Father: "The Lord wanted me to tell you that you are not loving Shiloh where she is." She continued, "She doesn't feel your love for her. She knows when you look at her you look right past her."

This took me by surprise but as I contemplated it, I realized that every time I talked with Shiloh, I would only see her as my little girl who loved Jesus or the adult prodigal who would return. I never loved her for who she had become. She had told me earlier in the summer that she was an atheist. I couldn't take it. She had gone from loving kids' church and VBS to wanting to be a missionary as a teenager to denying God's existence five years later.

I wrestled with being able to see her. I wanted so much for her. I wanted her to thrive. I wanted her to see that the beauty in her was the life of Christ shining through. I wanted to worship together as adults. I wanted to take my future grandkids to church and tell them Bible stores. For me, love was God. And if she didn't have God, she didn't have love. And if she didn't have love, how could I love her? That was how my disturbed mind was computing: God = love. No God = no love. Simple math turned wrong.

Chapter 35

Going Back Home

As I continued making good strides with my mental health through deconstructing myself, I realized the next step would be the rebuilding project. I still had a desire to unlock my childhood memories. I just knew that if I discovered the truth about those early years, I could make greater progress toward healing: "I want to go back to my childhood homes and see if any memories surface," I told Caleb one day. He thought it was a really good idea. He knew I was still struggling with empty spaces in my mind and if it would help, he was all for it. I planned to go at the beginning of April, just a few weeks from when I told him. I was looking forward to having some time apart. I knew this break would be good for our marriage. I hoped Caleb would be able to have a respite while I was gone

I hopped on a plane and headed for Chandler, Illinois, about 20 miles south of Peoria Briarfield. I had lived there in the middle school years while my dad had his first bout of cancer. I went to the church and hoped I would feel something. The church structure was the same on the outside but inside, some changes had been made—but the sanctuary remained the same. I gazed at the platform where my father preached from 35 years earlier. I looked over at where the piano had been and remembered learning how to play *What a Friend We Have in Jesus.*

Though these memories resurfaced, they weren't the answers I was looking for. I was looking for a memory to surface that would make sense of my bulimia, my suicide ideation, my depression, and my mental breakdown. In my mind, it had to be sinister, something like sexual abuse or a secret that the family kept from me. It would take something heavy like that to balance the scales. It couldn't only be that Margaret from the second grade stole my homework and claimed it was hers. So as I traveled from one place to another, I kept a record of it: what I was feeling, where I was visiting, who I was talking with. I was depending on God to lead me. If I was going to come face to face with the truth it would have to be on God's terms, not mine.

I went to my middle school and sat in the parking lot. Looking at the building I had spent two years in, I tried to remember anything that would connect some dots. I remembered where the long hallways were, especially the one where two boys were throwing fists. I saw the library where I was first introduced to a computer. I walked up to the glass doors and got buzzed in. I had no idea what I would say. I had no clue as to what I was looking for. I had hoped just seeing the building would unlock some memories.

"Hi, my name is Alora. I went to middle school here in 1986. I was hoping I could walk around with a staff person and just reminisce," I ignorantly asked. I knew times had changed. Security today was not like it was during my middle school days. From the days of walking the halls to wanting to walk them again, school shootings had quadrupled.

"I'm sorry, but no one is available to walk with you," she replied.

"I understand. Thank you anyway," I said disappointed.

I walked back to my car and caught a whiff of something that reminded me of elementary school. I knew smells had the ability to recall memories so I thought about that smell. *What is that?* I asked myself. Just then, I realized it was glue, but it wasn't like white, pasty Elmer's glue. Nor was it a glue stick. This smell was some sort of liquid adhesive. I couldn't think of the name of it, but I knew what it looked like. It came in a small bottle with an applicator brush. My next stop was to go to Wal-Mart to try and find it.

Spirit-Led

I spent a lot of time in prayer during this trip. I wanted to be led the whole time. I knew if I was going to remember anything, I was going to be led to it. So I walked down the office supplies aisle and looked intently on each shelf until I saw it: Elmer's rubber cement. That was exactly what I was looking for. I bought a bottle of it and then walked back to my car. The plan was that I would get back to the hotel room and open the bottle, inhaling the scent and wait. It was like following breadcrumbs.

Sadly, the smell didn't resurface any memory. I was just as blank as I was before my trip.

"God, I know You're here. I know You're leading me on this journey. Please reveal whatever it is that You want me to know," I prayed. At the time, I was thinking of memories. But God had other news for me. However, I wouldn't be privy to this information until the day before my trip was over.

I spent three days in Illinois. I found myself a nice coffee shop and began to write. I had bought a new journal for my trip. I have about 10 unfilled journals. Even though I am a writer, I'm terrible at journaling. But I had lots of time and I was on a mission. I needed a place to download my thoughts and emotions. But at times, I was just as blank as my mind. While there, I enjoyed a white mocha and was still waiting on God. There was nothing much to say. So I sat and read a book. I needed the time to myself and I needed time away from my triggers.

Triggered

I discovered I had many triggers that would go off at the slightest provocation. I began to identify when I would get triggered so I could try and avoid it. Caleb was still, if not more, involved in the life of the church. He was meeting with key leaders daily and finding safety at the church rather than at home. As he was getting more involved, I was shrinking in the background. I wanted to hide, to melt away. This feeling had been felt before. It was in the throes of anorexia when I would want to dissolve. I felt if I got skinny enough, I would be invisible.

By the time I had left for Illinois and California, I was encountering some sort of trigger every other day. In the beginning, I had no idea what was going to evoke a response. And when I was triggered, all I wanted to do was hide. However, over time I began to take notice of what was going on when I felt triggered. I began to compile a list of things that would typically set me off.

Then I discovered a pattern to my emotions that would follow a trigger. It looked something like this: Being triggered would lead to anger. I would want to fight because I would feel alone, misunderstood, and unheard. That would lead to anxiety. Fear was the source of my anxiety which made me want to run away and hide. Depression would set in after the anxiety would wear off. I would feel hopeless and have suicidal thoughts. After a bout of depression, shame would rear its ugly head. This would look like guilt, remorse, and embarrassment. The only way the cycle would stop was if I felt my relationship with Caleb was secure again. But just when our marriage seemed to be getting better, I would be triggered again and the cycle would start over.

Before my trip, my paranoia was off the charts. Our marriage was so fragmented and I didn't see a way out. I stared in the bathroom mirror and beheld a barely recognizable shell of myself, I thought about downing all my anti-depression meds. The same hopelessness I had felt 30 years earlier had reappeared: *Caleb would be better off without me*, I whispered to my soul. I was at a fork in the road. Looking back now, I wonder if my angel cried? Had this been as far as he could protect me? Had my life done a 360? Just then, I cried out to Caleb.

"Caleb, I need you," I cried.

Coming up the stairs he answered, "I'm here. What's wrong?"

"I need you to take me to the hospital. I don't want to live anymore," I wept.

I can only imagine what went through his mind. I had put him through so much pain over the previous three months. There I was laying a burden on him that was too heavy for anyone to bear. "Talk to me. What's going on?" he said, sounding concerned.

"I've ruined us and I think you'd be better off without me in your life," I continued to sob.

"We're going to be okay. Let's call the suicide hotline and get you some help," he gently replied, as always staying by my side.

I talked with a man and he helped me off the ledge so to speak. He got me connected to a local psychiatrist that same day. He was confident outpatient therapy would work for me. I got right in and was put on some medication that helped with my paranoia. This drug was the impetus for my healing.

After I spent three days in Illinois, I jumped back on the plane headed for San Francisco. The plan was to spend a few days in Santa Elia, about 45 minutes north and then three days in Crescent City, the small town I grew up in, which was six hours north of Santa Elia. All along, I was following God. I had no agenda except to go to my schools and houses we lived in. Other than that, I was listening for the Holy Spirit to lead me. If

He would reveal anything, I wanted to make sure I could hear Him, so I took lots of walks and sat in lots of coffee shops. I listened to worship music and I journaled. I found myself at the ocean and among the redwoods. The beauty all around was breathtaking. The idea of wanting my memories unlocked started to take a backseat to the love I was feeling from and for the Father. I had never felt so loved in all my life. It was palatable. I felt like I could reach out and hold it. It was so real. No longer had love been a fleeting emotion attached to neediness, but rather a gift like no other.

I began to weep as I felt the love of the Father cover me like a warm blanket. This kind of affection for me was transformative. My insecurities dissolved. The only thing that mattered in that moment was that I had tasted true love for the first time and I basked in it for hours. I realized love was going to be the answer to all my problems. I felt like I had been set free. The enemy no longer had a grip on me. I had been given new life and I was excited to get back home and share my revelation with Caleb. I texted Caleb, "I realized I can live without you. I don't want to but I can. God is enough for me." This was life-altering for me. I had become so co-dependent on Caleb for my worthiness. Now I was understanding worthiness from God in a whole new way.

"I'll be home around 2 p.m.," I told Caleb, excited to start our lives again.

"Ok, but just so you know I have a meeting at 7 p.m. tonight," he replied. Instantly the same feelings came over me. I was once again in competition and the church was winning. I was furious.

"You knew I was coming home. Why wouldn't you reschedule it? Why wouldn't you want to spend time with me?" I immediately felt abandoned. And Caleb instantly felt his walls go back up.

I got back home and instantly started picking a fight. I had been triggered by him saying he had a meeting. Just then I cried out. "There is something inside of me that needs to die. I don't know what it is, but it needs to come out!"

"Do you think you're resentful of the church?" he asked, trying to help me.

The lightbulb lit up like a Christmas tree. "Yes! That's exactly what is going on," I shrieked. I had been holding onto so much resentment dating back to my childhood with my dad being a pastor. I had no idea each brick of resentment had built up a fortress that kept me fighting truth, God, and Caleb.

"Can you call an elder and see if he can pray over me?" I asked, not caring who was going to find out. I just knew I needed help. A few minutes later I found myself being prayed over and anointed with oil. I confessed my resentment and was moved to tears. The chain that kept me in bondage had finally broken. I was free. I literally felt the weight fall off my shoulders. This was the end. I had come to a place of complete release from captivity.

Chapter 36

The Birth of POP

Prayer had become a big part of my life. Five years earlier I had found myself walking the church parking lot in Millhaven during the Sunday School hour praying for the congregation. I had felt there was a disconnect from what the church was saying and what they were doing. They would all agree that prayer was important, but they wouldn't show up for prayer meetings. They would lead us in worshipful music but I wondered if they truly believed the words they were singing. There was holy huddles and a lack of interest in newcomers coming to the church. So there I was every Sunday walking and praying and crying for the life of this church.

God has a beautiful way of placing burdens on His children for the sole purpose of having them do something about it in the power of the Holy Spirit. And so the desire to write a study on prayer developed. It began one Sunday morning when a parishioner came up to me and gave me a small pamphlet.

"Hi Alora. I got this in the mail the other

day and thought of you. Would you like it? It's a small book on prayer," Betty said, ever so sweetly.

Betty and her husband, Joseph, had a heart for the Lord. They would do anything for others and they were genuine.

She continued, "It's from the Catholic Church but I still think it has some great teaching."

"Thank you so much, Betty," I replied.

This had to be from God. Why would someone think to give me a book on prayer from a Catholic perspective? How did she know I had been burdened with praying for the church? God was up to something. I read the whole thing from cover to cover that same day. It was pretty brief but this became a seed God would grow in me.

The Introduction

I began writing the introduction and it captured my bleeding heart on paper. I wanted my readers to know the genesis of writing a study on prayer. The words just flowed from my heart onto the page. Here's what the Lord gave me:

> Maybe your understanding of prayer is much like mine was not too long ago. I defined prayer as time set aside to talk to God. Not a bad understanding and in most churches, it is the default posture of prayer. However, on the surface, this understanding of prayer often left me believing I was never praying as often as I should, as long as I should and as deep as I should. I left many prayer times feeling more guilt than freedom, more anxiety than peace, and more empty than filled.

I decided that if I believed the Scriptures to be true, than there had to be something wrong with my understanding of prayer. Because Philippians 4:6-7 tell us, "Do not be anxious about anything, but in every situation, by prayer and petition, with thanksgiving, present your requests to God. And the peace of God, which transcends all understanding, will guard your hearts and your minds in Christ Jesus." So the math should equal this: A (Prayer) + B (God's Promises) = C (PEACE). So if I wasn't experiencing peace, then I had to be doing something wrong, because again if I believe Scripture to be true, God does not offer anything to us that He won't deliver on (John 14:14).

What the Lord revealed to me was ironically summed up in my desire to control outcomes based on formulas apart from the leading of the Holy Spirit, focus on the Kingdom of God, and keeping God at the center no matter the situation. And this revelation shattered the box I ultimately realized I had put God in. God cannot and will not be contained in man-made ideologies created to pacify our own need to make human sense out of supernatural activity. The moment we try to make sense of mysteries we were never meant to understand (Proverbs 3:5-6) is the moment we begin building fences around our theology, enslaving us to our own deficient understanding of God.

So I found freedom in God and in that freedom, God revealed prayer is more than a one-sided conversation. It's being still, it's praising Him, it's singing to Him and about Him. It's collaborating in spiritual warfare, it's surrendering, it's following the Spirit's lead, it's repentance, it's forgiveness, it's meditating on Scripture. It's interceding for others, it's asking and it's waiting—and it's all laced in thanksgiving delivered with a grateful heart.

In summary, prayer is a gift designed to collaborate with the living God. As we work with Him, we are exposed to His character and will not only for our lives, but for our communities and world. He desires that we grow in our relationship with Him so He can use us to accomplish much. We need to be ready to listen when God speaks and bold to move when He says go. Prayer will attune our ears to His voice and give us confidence in Him that He is with us, no matter where He sends us. Jesus said in John 10:27, "My sheep listen to my voice; I know them and they follow me." Empowered by the Holy Spirit, the prayer of a righteous man can do much (James 5:16b).

I understand we all approach prayer in different ways. No one specific way is better than another, however, variety in your prayer life can ignite passion and renew vigor. Just like in relationships, if you do the same thing again and again, it can become dull and stale. And this can be true of our relationship with God. It's time to have a divine expectation that God has already shown up and desires to move in all situations. God wants us to approach Him with desire, anticipation, and faith. Our growth comes when we see the hand of God move and recognize our role in it.

I invite you to join me on this twelve-week journey of exploring and experiencing prayer in new and exciting ways! Together, we will embark on a quest for deeper understanding of who God is and who we are in light of Him. You will neither see God the same way nor experience Him as usual. Get ready to be amazed as your capacity to love others increases while your love for God expands.

And from there the study was written. It took me about three months to write it. I was driving one day on the highway when all of a sudden the word 'POP' entered my mind as a title for the book. *Pray on Purpose*. It stuck, and from there I began to envision teaching this curriculum. It started off as a two-day workshop. We had 12 people join the class. I was nervous but knew God was there and would provide the words I needed to share. My burden was that those present would begin to see prayer in a more expansive light, and that they would eventually have a stronger relationship with the Lord.

With every class, the teaching was expanded. The Holy Spirit kept downloading more material for the book. I would be taking a walk in our neighborhood and God would start speaking. I would get out my phone and open up the notes app and start typing while saying, "God, slow down. I can't write this fast!" It was a sweet time of clearly hearing from the Lord.

By the time I was struggling with my mental breakdown, I had lead the class five times. And even during the paranoia, anxiety, and fear, God would teach through me. Sometimes the class was more for me than for those in attendance.

Chapter 37

The Fall

Life had finally settled down. We had gotten through the girls trauma, a big fight with the kids we would later refer to as Niagara, and my mental breakdown. I was almost back to "normal." I had done so much work in therapy and my own personal deconstructing and rebuilding project. Our marriage slowly began to heal while we found trust again with each other. The girls had found themselves struggling so they moved in with us. We had a full house and a full heart. I was enjoying teaching POP and getting more involved in discipleship of women.

Caleb had been so busy all summer. He had just gotten back from the Dominican Republic for a mission's trip. We finished VBS at the church and celebrated with ten kids who had given their lives to Jesus. He was back in school for his doctorate and traveling to New York for classes once a quarter. With the year we had had, he was depleted. I had been begging him to not be so involved in the church but I wasn't convincing, probably because my motives were selfish. I wanted Caleb home to spend time with me. He really just needed rest, both physically and spiritually.

"I need to tell you something, Alora," Caleb said shortly after he got back from New York.

"Ok, what's up?" I said, expecting to hear something about our future. I always knew when he would want to talk about changes. His voice would change. He would sound very serious.

"On Monday night, while I was sitting in my hotel room, I received a message from someone I didn't know. She said she was lonely and started flirting with me. I asked her where she lived and she said New York. We left Messenger and went into SnapChat. Next thing I knew we had exchanged naked photos of each other," he said as flat as could be.

"Yeah right. You're joking," I said, not believing what he was saying.

"I wish I was, but I'm not," he said calmly.

Just then life was changed forever. We would be faced with more attacks and more trauma. But this time it would be at the hands of Caleb. Instantly, I was filled with strength.

"I'm so sorry. If you want to hit me or leave me, I would understand. Do whatever you want to do," he said, completely vulnerable.

"I forgive you. I love you. I'll stand by you no matter what," I responded. I had complete peace. Later I would struggle if what I had felt was numbness. In fact, I would write about numbness and peace being so similar—but I knew I meant those words.

I continued, "You were there for me when I went through my breakdown and paranoia.

And I'm going to be there for you through your mistake."

"Thank you. I love you so much. I'm so sorry," he said, on the verge of tears.

"I know you're just hearing this now but I have wrestled with this all week. I think we need to tell the girls, the elders, and the district. It doesn't seem right not to say anything. I don't trust myself to make any decisions, so I need your help," he added.

Fear immediately kicked in. It was fine that he sinned against me and God and that we both forgave him. In a way, I felt like we were even. But to make this public scared me to death. We were coming up on our one year anniversary of Niagara with the girls and I was so scared to lose them again. We were living in the parsonage so if he resigned, we'd have to move. But he was convicted that he needed to come public with his fall.

"Ok, let's tell them. I'll stand by your side the whole way," I said, assured yet knowing we were risking it all.

Risky Business

We called the girls in and told them everything. We had no idea how they would react. We knew they weren't following our same values of grace and forgiveness, at least from the biblical perspective. But we were trusting God would redeem this sin.

"You're disgusting," Shiloh said. That's all she could muster up.

"How could you cheat on mom? You need to leave!" Brenna shrieked. She was visibly shaking and getting red. She was definitely feeling this more than Shiloh. Shiloh was disappointed in dad but not angry with him to the same extent Brenna was.

"I don't want him to leave. We'll get through this. We love each other," I snapped back.

Brenna was upset with me because she thought I should leave Caleb. At the very least, I should make him spend the night in a hotel that night. But this was not her decision. I wasn't asking for advice. Our relationship was almost healed from the year prior and this just ripped our wounds back open. It was horrible.

Caleb called the elders and set up a meeting. All four of us went. The girls wanted to make sure he told them everything. They wanted him to pay for his sin. Brenna told Caleb that if he didn't resign, she wanted nothing to do with him. She didn't think he deserved to ever preach again. Again fear welled up in me and without praying about it, I told Caleb he had to resign. It wasn't worth losing his girls over it. And because Caleb was unable to trust himself, he did whatever I told him.

I thought the girls would be satisfied with Caleb falling on his sword, but they weren't. They were still disgusted and wanted nothing to do with him. And because I wasn't burning him at the stake, I was to blame as well. Shiloh began to make plans to move out while Brenna demanded she get to stay in the parsonage since it wasn't her sin that caused him to resign. They were both handling this devastation so differently and I didn't know which one was worse. I didn't know who would be harder to reconcile with.

The next step was to talk with the district superintendent. A meeting was scheduled for later on in the week. All Caleb's hard work of school, ministry, and ordination were threatened. What would the district say? What punishment awaited him? After a three-hour interrogation, Caleb was suspended for one year. His license was revoked so he couldn't serve for the next 12 months. To Caleb, this was a break he needed. He almost had the same response after the girls said they wanted a six-month break. He knew he was broken and needed to heal. The time away from the pulpit would later be a blessing.

But I was lost. I had found such purpose in ministry, and I had many friends within the church who provided support and love. We would have to find a new home, a new church, a new job, and a new community. But I had hoped we'd have the support of our friends to lean on.

The whole ordeal was a whirlwind. We went from one Sunday being perfectly fine to resigning the next Sunday. We were told we could take a few minutes after church to say goodbye but then that was it. We left out the back door. I felt like I had 13 years earlier after getting fired from the bank. The same feeling of defeat flooded over me. It would be a long journey of healing for our family but one that God would walk with us on.

Chapter 38

The Courtroom

I was numb. If I was at peace, I would have joy but there was nothing, but a blank slate. I didn't feel anything. But I did know God was working below the surface. I pleaded with Him once again.

> "God, are you there? Do you hear my shallow cries for something, anything, that will make all of this suffering make sense? I know You use the dark nights of the soul to transform, strengthen, and mold us more into Christ's likeness. But You have to know that numbness comes when the mind can no longer process the pain. Isn't that when You should stop the testing, cease the pressure, or at least give me time in between each heartache to process? I'm not telling You how to do Your job because You are very good at it, but I am suggesting this is too much. I'm pleading with you to relent. God, I know You're for me so why does it feel like You've turned Your

back on me? Is it because You don't like to see the suffering on Your children's faces? Please come to my rescue and restore my joy. Amen."

Responding, God opened the door that connected my heart to my mind. And instantly I was able to process my confusion though words. Here's an excerpt from my journal:

*****

Can I be honest with you? There are times where the last thing I want to do is pray much less the first thing. I find that when I've been hurt by others, I just want to isolate—isolate from the world and from God. I find great comfort in being with my husband, Caleb. He alone is my rock, my friend. I can trust him with my entire being. He is always for me and will never leave me. These are promises God tells me about Himself, but for some reason I believe Caleb more than I believe God. I see Caleb. I hear Caleb. I'm comforted by his arms. With God, all I feel is fear. Fear that if I don't do enough, I'll disappoint. And fear that if I get too close, Satan will be on my heels. It's dangerous to follow Jesus. The question I'm wrestling with is, Is it worth it?

The craziest thing in all of this is the one person who caused the loss, the pain was Caleb. He's the one who stepped outside the lines of our marriage. And yet, I've never been angry with him. I instantly forgave him, quickly showing him grace. And I had a strong desire to continue trusting him 100%. I don't know where that response came from. Just a few months earlier, I was paranoid he was happier with other people. I feared he would leave me and stop loving me. Ironically nothing was going on besides Caleb's overextended calendar. So why when something tangible happens, I react opposite? I don't get it. And this is where I need to start my journey.

Who is the real culprit? God for allowing Caleb to continue with his sinful choice? Caleb for falling into temptation? Me for not being enough for Caleb? The girls for making Caleb's life so difficult he needed a release from responsibility? The elders for not checking in and protecting him? The church for not recognizing Caleb's overextended schedule causing burnout? Caleb's parents for allowing abuse and neglect to go on for years? Or Satan who wanted nothing more than to see God lose by crippling a healthy church winning souls?

Was God at fault? This is a possibility. He is so powerful. But as I read His word, I see sin continues even after Jesus' warning? I see Jesus warning Judas before he betrays Him. I read Jesus giving Peter a heads-up that he would deny Him. He tells His disciples that the Spirit is willing but the flesh is weak. So though God can do anything, our freewill (that He ordained) supersedes His intervention. First Corinthians 10:13 tells us,

> No temptation has overtaken you except something common to mankind; and God is faithful, so He will not allow you to be tempted beyond what you are able, but with the temptation will provide the way of escape also, so that you will be able to endure it.

This tells me that even if we fall into temptation and sin He will provide a way of escape out of it. Why? Because He is faithful. He teaches us about sin, what it is and the consequences of it. He then gives us His Spirit to trigger warnings when we're getting too close to the edge. But then if we choose to still choose sin, He is faithful to show us a way out—He gives us a lifeline. So was God at fault? No.

Was Caleb at fault? This would make the most sense since he did the act. However, is he fully responsible for the entire loss and pain? What led to his fall? Burnout? Overextended schedule? Exhaustion? Depleted of the Spirit? No accountability? Isolation? Curiosity? Rebellion? I would imagine all of the above contributed somewhat to his choice. So was Caleb at fault? Yes, but I can understand his humanity got the better of him.

Was I at fault? The winter before Caleb's fall was the hardest on our marriage by far. I had been fighting my own battles. I had been repeatedly triggered when Caleb spent time at the church and with people. I traced it back to my father always being gone with the church and helping other people, while his family was fragile. I remember feeling like I didn't matter and that my own struggles were being overlooked.

So when I began feeling like Caleb cared more about the church and raising up leaders, I lost it. I took the insecurities birthed from my childhood into my adulthood and began fighting to save myself. I neither had the tools nor the voice to fight as a child. Now as a grown women, I wasn't going to be overlooked. I knew that kind of pain and I didn't want to relive it. So I fought.

However, this didn't endear Caleb to come closer but rather run from me. He built walls, created boundaries, and ran into the arms of the church. This went on for months. I realized six months later I was holding onto bitterness and resentment against the church. As soon as I confessed my sin to an elder and his wife, I felt released from the bondage. The chains fell and our relationship began to heal. But the wounds were already deep. The trust was already lost. It took months after this before Caleb could trust me fully. Before he could lower his walls. Boundaries remained in place.

So was I at fault. I think I was. So who am I to be upset at Caleb for being pushed out? I'm just as culpable for his fall as he was. If he forgave me for my dysfunction, the least I could do is forgive him for his misstep. What I gave him was what he gave me—grace and mercy. I basically accused him of having an affair for four months. He exchanged one photo to a stranger. I don't even think we're even.

Were the girls at fault? We had a huge falling out with our girls the summer before, a year to be exact. It had taken about six months before they began to come back around, then another three months of repairing the relationship. We were coming up on our one-year anniversary and I was wanting to do something special. Losing them was the most painful time in my life. Hurting them devastated us. We had been drifting apart the last three years in our values system. We still loved them but had nothing in common anymore. Both girls walked away from the faith.

It was and is still so painful not to share our lives together in harmony. My relationship with God was uprooted and everything became a battle. It felt like I was in a tug of war. I went from defending God to them to understanding why they left. I find myself doubting His goodness even today. So were the girls at fault for Caleb's fall? No. But they were at fault for the pain that came in the days, weeks, and months that followed.

How I choose to respond to Caleb was painful for the girls, mainly Brenna. She just didn't understand why I wasn't mad, why I didn't kick him out. But looking back, I was numb and had no feeling. It was almost like my heart was amputated. All I knew was that I needed Caleb. Everyone showed me that they can easily leave when things get bad. And even though I pushed Caleb away, he never left. Were the girls responsible for us leaving the church? I truly believe they were. Brenna demanded Caleb resign. Our relationship was held hostage by this demand. Fearing another Niagara (when the girls walked away), I folded. I never consulted God. I responded in fear. So I told Caleb to quit. And because he left next steps up to me, he did. Looking back, I would've taken more time to think, reason, and pray about it. Maybe things would be different today if I didn't act so hastily.

Were the elders at fault? Did they drop the ball by not checking in with Caleb? Did they fail to provide accountability? Did they accept Caleb's resignation too soon? Were they wrong to accept it at all? Did they not pray enough for protection against the enemy? Did they too fall prey into the enemy's hands by letting Satan win, to have the victory of taking out the tip of the spear? Could this have been handled differently? Could more love, grace, and mercy been showed? I believe so. Do I think they are at fault for Caleb's fall? I believe to some extent they were. They were definitely culpable for the pain that followed.

The hardest to believe was everyone scattered like the disciples on the night Jesus was betrayed. Everyone left. Caleb was given five minutes to explain his resignation and ten minutes to say goodbye before leaving through the back door. Could the elders have reasoned with the district about how that Sunday would go down? Could we have been invited to the ice cream social that followed where the congregation could ask questions? Did they continue to pray for him? Did they cut off the friendship when Caleb's ministry there was buried? Is Caleb just another replaceable spokesperson for God? Didn't his friendship matter? Was he just another failed pastor people would talk about in the coming months?

So again, were the elders at fault? I believe they became culpable to his future fall when Caleb told them point blank, "Guys, I feel like I'm either burning out or headed towards clinical exhaustion." And they responded with, "We'll pray for you pastor." Not, "What can we do to help ease your load? What can I take off your plate?"

Was the church at fault? It's hard to say a collective group of people should know the pressures their pastor was experiencing. The church would not know his schedule but maybe his assistant would have. Could she have said something?

How appropriate would that have been? Did she notice how busy he was, how invested he was in the bride of Christ? Did that bother her? If so, did she mention her concerns to anyone—the elders, her friends? Looking back, I was probably the only one who noticed. But Caleb wasn't taking my advice since it was laced with fear and paranoia. But I do find fault with the church after the resignation. At the time Caleb resigned, the church came up to us and hugged and loved on us. They promised they would keep us in prayer and that everything would be okay. Did I take that demonstration of love as a way our lives would be?

Looking back over the last five months and only a handful of people reaching out, I realized that day was our funeral and that outpouring of love was the procession of mourners. I was naive to think this love would cover a multitude of sins, much less one. But I guess Caleb's fall was greater than theirs. I never would have believed this church family would shun us. And that is where the pain comes from—a church family that said they would be there for us and when we left, they did as well.

Were Caleb's parents at fault? For decades, Caleb chose to ignore the scars and unaddressed wounds from the abuse he encountered as a child. He was able to compartmentalize his childhood from his adulthood. He packaged up his ability to be successful and unaffected as resilient. I was astounded at this ability to be able to come out of that childhood unscathed, unmoved, and "normal." His abuse didn't compare to my abuse and yet I was a mess—and in some ways, I still am. I spent decades numbing my pain with bulimia, then years in counseling trying to heal the little girl who was damaged. Why did things not affect Caleb? How was he able to live life devoid of scars?

But then Niagara happened and like the rush of the waterfalls came the crack in a lifetime of resiliency. He knew his past was catching up with him and that he had to deal with it—the abuse, the secrecy, the shame, the abandonment. He began counseling a few weeks after the incident and within a few months he was done. His counseling fixed him or at least he thought. A lifetime of dysfunction fixed with eight therapy sessions! Maybe naivete resulted in his fall or the unguarded layers of his recently opened up wounds. So were his parents at fault for his fall? I would say no. Though they contributed to his foundation, Jesus traded that one in for a piece of his cornerstone.

Was Satan at fault? This is the easiest one to place blame on. He hates God's children. He seeks to kill, steal, and destroy. He is the father of lies, distortion of light, and a champion of the flesh. When God loses, he rejoices. The day Caleb fell, the church fell and I know Satan was jubilant. He sets us up with temptation and offers us satisfaction of the flesh. He is by far the right one to place blame on. But was it all Satan? Could Caleb have fought against him and won? Could Caleb have called on God to intervene? Satan set the table but did Caleb have to sit and eat? Satan was at work earlier in our ministry. He tried multiple times to get me. And most often he did. He affected my relationships, my ministry, and my life. I believe his plan was always to get Caleb but started with me to weaken Caleb. I definitely blame Satan.

Will attaching blame to the right person make things better? Will my trust ever be rebuilt back up to withstand the next chapter in our lives? Do I need people to pay for Caleb's sin? Is a shared blame the thing that will heal my wounds? Caleb is paying for his sins. He was suspended from ministry for a year. He has work to do every month and at the end of the year, his case will be reviewed. Will he be restored back into the ministry? Or will he have to pay for his sins forever? Our lives have been uprooted. New place, new job, new church, new friends. I'm living in transition unable to put roots down. I've lost friends through all this. The pain is constant and its effects are unending. How do I move on? How do I look forward to the future? What does the future hold to be happy for anyway? How does one heal from a complicated, layered, ongoing wound?

*****

This journal entry was written in 2023 and now we are fine. We are better than fine. Our relationship with the girls have been restored. We are stronger than ever. Caleb was reinstated back into full-time ministry. About three months later, he accepted a lead pastor position in Erie, Pennsylvania. Looking back now, God was always there, always working even when it didn't seem like it. God was healing our hearts and wounds. His timing is perfect. When Caleb accepted the offer to minister at ELRAC, he felt whole again. I felt whole again. I am no longer ashamed. I am no longer living in fear. I have confidence in the Lord and His plans for us. We are living proof that man can fall and get back up again redeemed, restored, and renewed.

Chapter 39

The Sacred Place

Sitting on the couch recently, discussing my car accident with Caleb, he asked me a question that forever changed my perception of God. "What if God didn't push you off the cliff? What if you just fell asleep at the wheel because you only had two hours of sleep? And instead, what if God jumped in to rescue you?"

My mind was blown. All this time I believed God pushed me off the cliff to get my attention and get me back in line. I was fearful of and intimidated by God so I tended to keep Him at a distance while developing my relationship with Jesus and the Holy Spirit only. But with that change of perspective, I could see His love and care for me. And then He gently whispered, "I didn't send my angel to rescue you. I chose to rescue you Myself!"

He held me as I flew off the cliff. He sheltered me as I hit the water. He embraced me as I sank to the bottom. And He lifted me out of the wreckage. As I pondered this new epiphany, I reflected on Psalm 40:2, "He drew me up from the pit of destruction, out of the miry bog, and set my feet upon a rock, making my steps secure."

On October 5, 2024, Caleb and I made our way to Clear Water, Wyoming in search of the place where my life was forever changed. It had been 32 years since that terrible, beautiful day. I always wanted to go back but never made it a priority, though I went back there many times in my mind. As we drove on the long stretch of road from Clear Water toward the ranch, I peered out the window as if looking for a lost child. I began to get anxious and nervous.

"Caleb, how do I know it was ten miles from the ranch?" I asked, questioning my 32-year-old truth.

"Well, for the last 26 years of you telling me this story, the details have never changed," he responded, trusting in my memories.

"But how did I actually know? I mean, I was literally in shock and was the only one at the scene," I continued, beginning to doubt my own truth.

"Five minutes," Caleb counted down, as we kept looking for the landmarks I knew for certain had to be there.

"Ok, I know it's on the left side of the road paralleling the Shoshone River heading toward the ranch. I know there is a telephone pole that I swerved to miss. I know there are boulder rocks and a cliff near the road. And it has to have a rocky island in the middle of the river," I described.

"One minute," Caleb continued.

"There, pull over there," I eagerly shouted as anxiety began to sneak up on me.

I got out of the car and looked around. There was a telephone pole on the left side but the river was past some brush and trees and about 50 yards off the road. If I was going 50 miles an hour, maybe I went through brush before falling off the cliff. But as I walked, it became clear to me this was not the spot.

"Is this the place?" Caleb asked, excited for me.

"No, let's keep going," I said, never questioning if I would find it but that it might be closer to the ranch.

We kept driving and saw another area that had potential. We got out the car and began walking around. I felt like I was trespassing. It wasn't my sacred spot. I prayed, "God please give me success today. Bring me to the place where You rescued me and changed my life."

"It's not here either. Let's keep driving," I said, fully confident we were close.

We went up another mile and rounded the corner and instantly I knew the place had just been uncovered. I felt it. "That's it, Caleb!" I asked him to pull over and got out.

Caleb had been suffering from sciatica and so he decided to stay in the car. He did so partly because he was in pain but also because he knew how special this ground was to me and he wanted to give me the space to be reunited with it.

There it was. The telephone pole. The gravel. The 30-foot cliff. The river. The rocky island. As I looked at the sight, I was shocked to realize the crash site was only 2.4 miles from the ranch. This was within walking distance to my troubled and lonely existence. Had I left three minutes earlier from Clear Water, I would've gotten safely to the ranch and my life would've continued going down a destructive path.

The telephone pole was another eye opener to the grace of my Lord. As I approached it, I realized it wasn't a standard wood telephone pole but rather a steel power pole. My car didn't have airbags. Had I not woken up and slammed into the pole, would I have walked away from that? I know God had a plan for my life and sparing it was the beginning of it. But as I felt the sturdy steel, I couldn't help but wonder if my miracle consisted of many micro-miracles, like waking up in time to swerve away from the pole.

I wanted to jump into the water. I couldn't get close enough to it. Going off the cliff and crashing on the rocks was the result of lack of sleep. But the waters are what decided my burial or my baptism. I wished to be captivated by the current again to feel the powers that fought for my life. God saved me. He physically pulled me out of the wreckage, though I didn't see Him. He lifted me up out of the cold and dark waters, though I didn't feel Him. He spoke to my scared and lonely heart, though I didn't hear Him.

How long do I stay? What do I take? What do I say? I know this place is sacred, but how does one approach such a moment? Do I memorialize it by building an altar? Do I speak over the waters? Do I touch the waters, the rocks, the dirt? Do I throw something in the water like it's a wishing well? Do I take a rock as a memento? What is the right posture? What is the right attire? Do

I kneel? Do I stretch out my arms upward? Do I sing? Do I remain silent? Do I take pictures? Do I not? These were questions that were racing through my mind.

I prayed to God a prayer of thanksgiving for saving my life that day. I knelt down and touched the water, grabbed a rock, and took a few pictures, And then I left. I felt like I was leaving a part of me behind, a part of me that needed to go back to the scene and remain. It was a part that was never meant to leave there in the first place. But what was it? And what was its purpose in remaining?

As we drove back to Billings, Montana, I felt nothing but peace and gratitude. One day I will be united with my Savior and watch the entire scene play out. That will be the day I will see perfectly, feel perfectly, and hear perfectly.

And I will be reminded of what I have learned: God was always there!

About the Author

Alora Stone is a writer and the founder of *Small Mountain Writing*. She writes under a pseudonym to protect the privacy of those in her story while remaining faithful to its emotional truth. Her work centers on faith, endurance, and redemption, with the purpose of bringing glory to God and creating spaces where the wounded can find comfort, strength, and hope through shared experience.

Alora resides in northwestern Pennsylvania with her husband and two adult daughters. Together, they pastor a C&MA church and enjoy life with their three blue heeler dogs. In addition to her writing, Alora co-owns and manages a tax and accounting firm.

What's Next

This is Alora's first published book. She has also written Bible study curricula on prayer and evangelism and has authored more than fifty articles that will be compiled into a devotional in 2026.